JAMES DICKSON and HIS LEGACY

Audrey Mitchell

KELSO
CAMEOS

Published by Audrey Mitchell, Fairview House, Nenthorn, Kelso, Scottish Borders TD5 7RY.

Printed in the Scottish Borders by Kelso Graphics.

Cover Picture: Ednam House c.1820 by an unknown artist, kind permission of Mr and Mrs Alastair Brooks.

This book is gratefully dedicated to
Alastair and Sheila Brooks
of Ednam House, Kelso.

CONTENTS

James Dickson 1712-1771

From the copy of the original Thomas Hudson portrait, kind permission of Mr and Mrs Alastair Brooks.

The artist Thomas Hudson (1701-1779) was fashionable as a portrait painter between 1740 and 1760. His best-known portrait, of George Frederick Handel, hangs in the National Portrait Gallery in London. Hudson's most famous pupil was Joshua Reynolds.

INTRODUCTION

The story of James Dickson, the saddler's apprentice who damaged the pantwell, or drinking-fountain, in the Square, ran off to London to avoid punishment and returned years later a wealthy man, is probably the best-known legend in Kelso. However, as research into his life and times progressed, it became clear that some of the information about him, handed down over two centuries, is quite inaccurate. For one thing, as there was never any mention of Mrs. Dickson, he was assumed to have been a bachelor. It wasn't until Sir Ilay Campbell, a keen collector of book-plates, wrote to ask if I could provide any information on "James Dickson of Ednam", whose arms were impaled with those of an unidentified lady, that his marriage came to light. Betty Hogg survived her husband and remained in Kelso for a number of years, but her name is not included on his tombstone in Ednam Kirkyard so she may eventually have returned to London.

Ednam House was originally known as Havannah House, recalled today in the name of an adjacent court. It was thought that the name derived from a treasure ship captured by James Dickson, but the Maritime Information Centre at Greenwich has no record of a ship of that name until 1767, when a brig called "Havannah" was built in America. It is much more likely that the name was chosen in celebration of the victorious siege of Havannah, Cuba, in 1762. William Dickson, nephew to James, served under Sir George Pocock who commanded the naval fleet involved.

Kelso Races have been recorded as taking place over Caverton Edge near Morebattle as far back as 1735, but were not firmly established until the 1760s. Sir John Paterson, son-in-law of the Earl of Marchmont, ran his horse against another in the Races of 1765 and it was handsomely beaten. The victor was a grey horse named "Cheviot" ridden by Tommy Hudson and supposedly belonged to James Dickson. However, a respected race historian states that it is recorded that "Cheviot" was owned by Sir Alexander Don, a noted breeder of race-horses.

It has also been claimed that Dickson formed the "Bowmen of the Border", but this group was not instituted until 1788 by diploma from the Royal Company of Archers in Scotland, with Sir Alexander Don as a founder member. The number of members was restricted to 80 and they were commanded by first and second captains. Their meetings were held on the first Thursday of the month from May to November, on the 10th of January and the King's Birthday.

James Dickson owed his success as much to good fortune as to good management. Firstly, he attended school in Scotland, a country renowned for its education, whose young men were sought after for that very reason. Although very poorly paid, schoolmasters were themselves learned men, teaching languages, surveying and numeracy to a high standard. Secondly, the time when Dickson went to London was one of great and rapid economic growth and opportunity, in colonies both East and West. The Navy was expanding and with it the need for victuals and provisions of all kinds. A shrewd business-man, as Dickson must have been, found little difficulty in becoming rich, and with wealth came influence. The list of trustees appointed by Dickson to handle his affairs after his death includes some well-connected Borders gentry, indicating a social status for James Dickson which was apparently above that of his birth. The secret partly lies in their mutual membership of Masonic Lodges. Dickson had been Senior Grand Warden of England and was elected Royal Worshipful Master of the Lodge of Kelso, no. 58, on St. Andrew's Day, 1766. The Lodge had been in existence for many years, possibly as far back as 1658, and hitherto had met in premises owned by Mr. Winter or Mr. Fraser, but in November 1767 James Dickson offered them the use of a room in a tenement he was building. Their first meeting in the "Assembly Room", indicating that the new-built tenement was in fact the Cross Keys Hotel, took place two years later. James Dickson, still spending much of his time in London, was rarely present at these meetings and the chair was taken by a Past Master. On the feast of St. John the Baptist, 24th June 1769, the Lodge met and then walked to the "chappel for the service of the Church of England". This was St. Andrew's Episcopalian Church which was also newly built, on ground which had been owned by James Hardie, to the south of the gardens of

Ednam House. Richard Wallis, Vicar of Carham, had become Episcopalian pastor for Kelso in 1757 and as he too was a Freemason he preached to the Lodge.

Given that James Dickson's story must have been well-known to Sir Walter Scott, who was born in the year of Dickson's death, it might seem strange that he did not use this remarkable man's life as inspiration for a novel. Sir Walter's father was Dickson's solicitor and acted for him in many of his purchases of land or property, sometimes travelling to London with contracts to be signed. Sir Walter's elder brother, Robert, served in the Navy under Captain William Dickson, nephew and heir of James, and was in several of "Rodney's battles". Sir Walter himself gives the probable explanation: ...."although I have deemed historical personages free subjects of delineation, I have never on any occasion violated the respect due to private life".

James Dickson's wealth and enterprise commended him as a potential Member of Parliament. At that time several towns could be linked in one Burgh Constituency, and Linlithgow Burghs included Linlithgow, Lanark, Selkirk and Peebles. In the general election of 1768, John Lockhart Ross was returned for the seats of both Linlithgow Burghs and the shire of Lanark and opted for the latter, so on 29th December, 1768, James Dickson was elected unopposed for the Burghs seat. His short time in parliament seems to have been uneventful; he voted for the expulsion of Wilkes from the House of Commons in 1769 and he sided with the majority in divisions on the Middlesex election.

James Dickson's life was one of energy, diversity and benevolence. He took interest in a wide variety of subjects, from business to sport, from architecture to civil engineering. His proposal to form a canal between Ednam and Berwick was perhaps too novel an idea to attract support from canny Borderers. His death at the early age of 59 seems to have been unexpected and he was widely regretted. To those Kelsonians who are dismayed to learn that James Dickson was not the Romantic Pirate of their imagination, I offer apology and hope that his real story compensates by sheer interest!

Audrey Mitchell
June, 1997.

DICKSON FAMILY TREE - 1st GENERATION

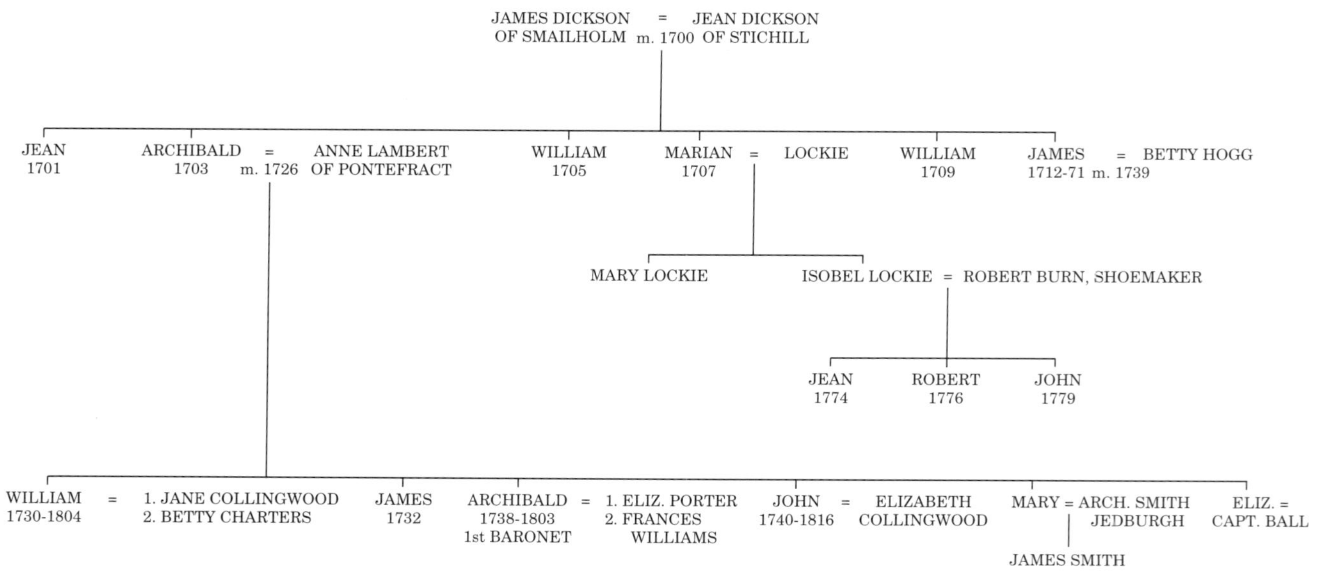

CHAPTER ONE

FAMILY

The village of Stichill lies in Roxburghshire, one of Scotland's border counties, about three miles to the north of the market town of Kelso. The ground rises towards Stichill and beyond, into the neighbouring county of Berwickshire, culminating in a rocky eminence surmounted by the prominent outline of Hume Castle, visible from miles around. Nestling beneath the Castle, the village of Hume was frequently affected by cross-border warfare and, perhaps as a result, its little church became ruinous during the seventeenth century. Despite being in different counties, the parishes were united to become Stichill and Hume in 1640 but retained distinct identities, each having its own parochial board and its own school.

The Pringle (or Hoppringill) family was to be found in many areas of the Border, and the Lairds of Stichill were descended from George Pringle of Newhall in Selkirkshire. His second son, Robert Pringle, bought the estate at Stichill in 1628 and when he died in 1649 he was succeeded by his grandson, also Robert. This young man had been left fatherless at a tender age and was brought up at Stichill House under the care of his uncle Walter, a loyal supporter of the Covenanting cause. Robert Pringle became a member of the Scottish Parliament in 1681 and a Baronet of Nova Scotia in 1683 (note 1). His successor in 1692 was his son, Sir John Pringle, who had married Magdalen Elliot of Stobs, south of Hawick.

From the time of Cromwell, every parish had its court of justice, under the jurisdiction of the local baron, "which took cognisance of debts, promises and trespass". The Baron Court of Stichill, under Sir John Pringle, met in the Kirk and the transactions were recorded in minute-books. In 1692, "Archibald Dickson made payment to George Hamiltone in the Hill £12.5.8 Scots (note 2) for the harvest fee", and in 1705 James Dickson, tenant in Parkend, was owed £30 Scots as the agreed price of "ane naig" (horse). Parkend lies on the western edge of the Stichill estate, near where Stichill House then stood. In 1727, an account was drawn up of the 40 husband-lands in Stichill and Parkend was noted as being "part of the ten lands in the Overtown, being an husband land and an half a quarter and a half quarter" *(sic)*. In those days, the salaries of the minister and school-master were paid from taxes levied on the proprietors or "heritors", and tenants. Parkend was rated for the schoolmaster's salary at £1.17.6. At Oxmuir, beside the village of Hume, lived William Dickson to whom, in 1715, £3 Scots was owed by Isobel Pringle; he died, an old man, in 1760. There were many people of the name Dickson living in the vicinity at the time and, unfortunately, it is now quite difficult to establish the relationship between the various families.

In 1700, on the 15th of February, Jean Dickson of Stichill was married to James Dickson of Smailholm by the Rev. John Glen. Standing as Jean's "cautioner" was James Lamb, while William Lillie stood surety for her bridegroom. As they shared the same surname, it is possible that Jean and James were already related - perhaps cousins. Settling at Stichill, their first child, Jean, was born the following year and their first son, Archibald, in 1703. The second son, William, born in 1705, probably died in infancy, as another William was christened four years later. (According to Scottish naming tradition of the time, this indicates that James was the son of Archibald and Jean was the daughter of William). Their second daughter Marion, or Mary Anne, born in 1707, married a Mr. Lockie in Kelso and had two daughters, the elder Mary and the younger Isobel, who married Robert Burn, shoemaker in Kelso.

In September 1712 was born the youngest son of James and Jean Dickson, named after his father. At the time of James' birth, Scotland was in an unsettled state following the Union of Parliaments with England, and the succession to Queen Anne was a subject of intrigue and dispute. After her death in August 1714, conflict escalated, the Jacobite cause was espoused by many and the Borders was often the scene of strife, including in 1715 a proclamation for King James VIII at the Market Cross in Wester Kelso. Armies passed through the district, foraging and plundering; muskets and broadswords were found in Hume Castle and a small quantity of gunpowder was found in the church. Sir John Pringle's horses were taken, his pewter was used to make bullets and his corn was burned.

The eldest son of the Dickson family, Archibald, left the troubled border area, set himself up as a baker in Pontefract, Yorkshire, and married Anne Lambert in 1726. They had six children, including four sons: William born 1730; James 1732; Archibald 1738; John 1740. Their daughter Mary married Archibald Smith of Jedburgh and had a son, James, while her sister Elizabeth married a Captain Ball.

Meanwhile, Archibald's youngest brother, James Dickson, was apprenticed to a saddler called Richardson in Kelso, a town which at that time consisted of two parts, Wester and Easter. Wester Kelso stood on the banks of the Tweed opposite the remains of the ancient Royal Burgh of Roxburgh, on a site now contained within the walls of Floors Castle. There was a road known as "the Common Way" (now Roxburgh Street) between it and Easter Kelso, which had grown up near the Abbey. A Market Square, which was unusually large for a Scottish town, was the central focus of Easter Kelso and was surrounded by unmade streets of thatched dwellings. There had been a disastrous fire in 1684 which destroyed many of these central buildings and a map was drawn up to show ownership of the ruined properties, with the name Dickson appearing at the corner of the Square and the Common Way, and again a few doors further to the north. Gradually the town was reconstructed and in 1696 a "Council House" fronting the Square was erected by the Countess of Roxburghe. Nearby stood the public drinking-fountain, or pantwell, and legend has it that James Dickson, no doubt in high-spirited mischief, vandalised the pantwell and fled to avoid punishment. Assuming that he was in his teens, it would have been around the time of Archibald's marriage and Pontefract would have been a convenient stopping-place en route for the South. Certainly the brothers were in close contact, for James treated nephew William as his heir, having no children of his own at the time of his death.

By 1739 James was living in London, in the vicinity of the Tower, and in that year he married Betty Hogg (who may have been daughter to one of several merchants of that name in the area) in St. Katherine-by-the-Tower. This church was of great antiquity, originally built in 1147 by Matilda, wife of King Stephen, in memory of her two sons who died in infancy, with a hospital for the poor alongside. The church and hospital remained as property of the Queens of

The Coronarium

England, a fact which prevented them being destroyed during the purges of Henry VIII. They were, however, demolished in 1825 to make way for St. Katherine's Dock, under the supervision of the Company's engineer, Thomas Telford. The site is now marked by a circular chapel, a domed roof resting on pillars, known as the Coronarium.

Dickson of Kilbucho and Hartree

James set up as a merchant in the Crutched Friars, a small winding street in the vicinity of the Tower, becoming increasingly wealthy. At the height of his prosperity, he adopted a coat of arms, azure with three mullets argent on a chief ermine three bezants or. There are obvious similarities to the arms of Dickson of Kilbucho and Hartree; the motto is the same, but the hand on the crest is replaced by an arm in armour. The Kilbucho Dicksons were descended from John Dickson, Lord Hartree and his first wife, Bessie Barbour, while the descendents of his second wife, Susanna Ramsay, whom he married in 1632, inherited Hartree. Lord Hartree and his brother, James, were grandsons of Robert Dickson and his wife, Anne Eccles, daughter of John Eccles of that Ilk. James was also married twice and his second wife was Margaret Edmonstoun, a surname well-known in Ednam. While it is tempting to speculate that these were direct ancestors of James Dickson of Ednam, this is open to conjecture (see Family Tree on page 60).

By kind permission of Sir Ilay Campbell

Betty Hogg's coat of arms, impaled with the Dickson arms on James Dickson's bookplate opposite, are incorrect, and the wild boar passant is at odds with the usual Hogg arms which display three boars heads. Neither Betty nor James had the authority of the Lyon Court to display in Scotland the arms shown here. Betty Dickson was named as one of the Trustees to her husband's will, survived him on his death in November 1771 and remained at Ednam House until 1787.

In July, 1768, James Dickson drew up a deed of entail in which he stipulated that his heirs should "constantly retain the surname, arms and designation Dickson of Ednam as their own proper and only surname; any female heir obliged to take the name for her husband". When James died, his heir was William Dickson, eldest son of his brother Archibald, who had joined the Royal Navy and was a Lieutenant by 1755, serving under Sir George Pocock, his commander during the Seven Years War. Eleven years later, he was promoted to Captain of the "Jersey", 60 guns, under Commodore Spry, and invested with chief command on the Gibraltar station. In November 1769, William wrote from the "Jersey" to acquaint the Commander of the Royal Navy that

> *"in coming out of Carrick Road near Falmouth, I had to leave a stream anchor and Hawser of 7" behind – had to cut it to avoid falling on board a Russian Ship of War".*

Commodore Spry left orders with Lt. Barron, commanding the fly cutter, to take up the abandoned gear and deliver it to the stores at Plymouth.

In 1777, William was appointed to the "Greyhound" frigate and served on the American station during the succeeding two seasons, before the ship returned for refitment. In 1779, when Spain joined France and the American colonies in a war against Britain, he was involved in the siege of Gibraltar prior to sailing to the West Indies with Sir George Rodney.

On return, he took command of the 64-gun "Sampson" before being transferred to the "Standard" which, being unready for war service, remained as a guardship at Plymouth. From 1793 onwards, William Dickson rose rapidly from rear-admiral of the Blue to Vice-admiral of the White, when he succeeded Sir Richard Onslow as commander of a division of the North Sea fleet; and finally to Admiral of the Blue. (note 3)

Meanwhile, William's brother Archibald had also joined the Royal Navy and not only attained the rank of Admiral of the Blue, but in 1802, the year before he died, had a Baronetcy of the United Kingdom conferred on him "in consideration of his professional services". He settled in Hardingham, Norfolk, was twice married and had a daughter, Elizabeth, by his first wife. Archibald would have been next in line as heir to his uncle James; he inherited £2,000 from him in 1771.

The youngest brother, John, went his own way to become a Lt.-General in the army, having signed up for the 68th Regiment of Foot.

The only one of Archibald's four sons to remain a civilian was James, who would appear to have been a coach-maker in London, as he was so designated in his uncle James' will when he was left £100. His name was omitted from the list of possible heirs, no reason given. Instead, failing all others, the estate was to go to James Smith, eldest son of Archibald Dickson's daughter Mary and her husband Archibald Smith, Jedburgh. Other beneficiaries in James Dickson's will were his sister, Mary Dickson or Lockie, who was granted £1,500 a year for life; her daughter Mary, who was to receive £100; her other daughter Isobel, wife of Robert Burn, also £100. Fred Vernon, in his book "Kelso Past and Present" says that his relative, John Stevenson, joiner in Stichill, was married to a niece of James Dickson who was thought to be "awfu' kind, but tremendous clarty". Unfortunately, her name is not mentioned.

The executors entrusted with carrying out James Dickson's wishes, besides his wife should she survive him, included some well-known figures in Border society: the Hon. George Baillie of Jerviswood; Walter Scott of Harden, Esq.; Sir James Douglas of Springwood Park; Col. George MacDougall *(sic)* of Makerstoun; Col. James Pringle of Stichill and Dr. William Ormiston of Hendersyde.

Admiral Cuthbert Collingwood

Two of James Dickson's nephews, William and John Dickson, married daughters of Alexander Collingwood of Unthank, near Whittingham in Northumberland. The Collingwoods were a well-known and numerous family, some of whom had supported the Jacobite cause. Admiral Cuthbert Collingwood was a member of the branch which had fallen into unfortunate circumstances after the Civil War in the 17th century and the rebellion of 1715. He was born in Newcastle and entered the Navy at the age of eleven. He served on several ships and in 1777 was tried by court-martial on a number of charges amounting to disobedience and neglect of duty, but acquitted. He assumed command of the "Badger" after his

CONNECTION BETWEEN DICKSON, COLLINGWOOD, KER AND PRINGLE

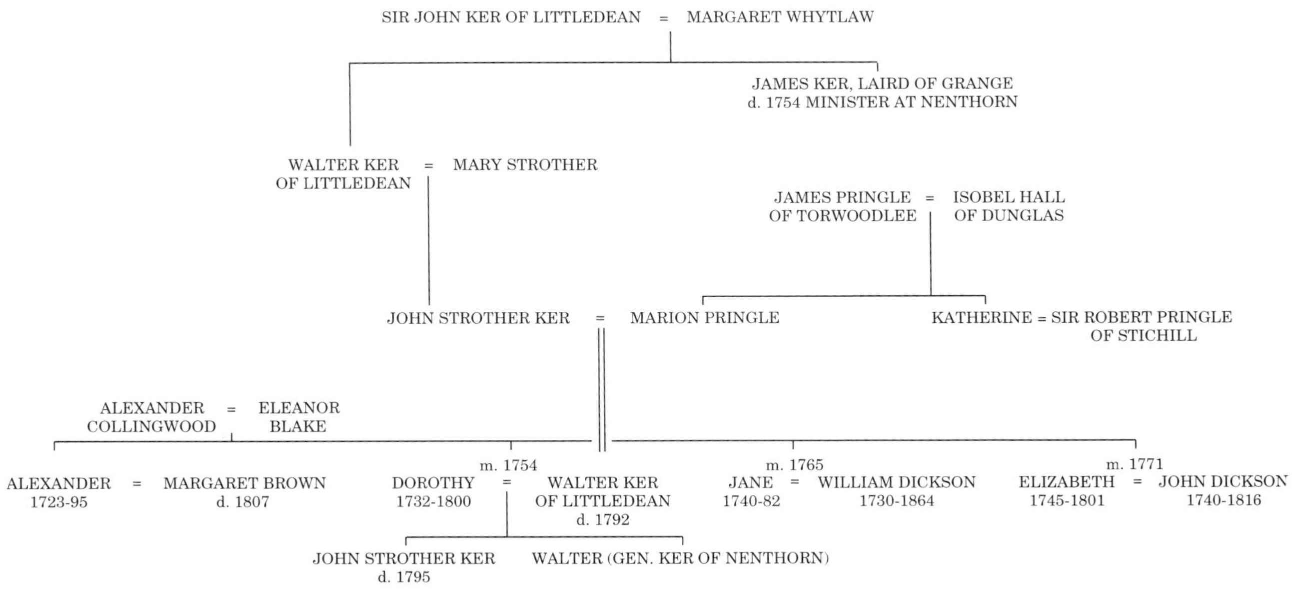

friend, Horatio Nelson, and overlapped in command of the "Sampson" with William Dickson. After several other commissions, Collingwood took part in the battle of Trafalgar, where he led the lee-line, and he took command of the fleet after Nelson's death. He was raised to the peerage as Baron Collingwood of Caldburne and Hethpoole.

His kinsman Alexander Collingwood, father-in-law to William and John, had been born in 1700 at an old bastle house called Little Ryle. Alexander's parents, Alexander Collingwood and Dorothy Lawson, built a small mansion house nearby and named it Unthank, later changed to Collingwood House; it was finally demolished by Lord Ravensworth around 1850. Alexander married Eleanor Blake, sister of Sir Francis Blake of Twizell, and they had fourteen children; six boys and eight girls.

In 1754, the oldest surviving daughter, Dorothy Collingwood, married Walter Ker, who not only owned an estate in Northumberland, being a descendant of the Strother family of Fowberry, but also held Littledean and Nenthorn in Berwickshire. He was related to the Roxburghe Kers on his father's side, and to the Pringles of Stichill on his mother's. A year after they married, Walter and Dorothy visited Sir Robert and Lady Pringle at a time when the Stichill minister, the diarist George Ridpath, was present. He noted: "Went to Sir Robert's with Nancy (his sister) where we found Littledean's people, younger and older. Saw the young beauty (Dorothy) who has a pretty face, also a neat little person. But her face scarce expresses anything but pertness, her voice coarse, her manner of speaking rapid and disagreeable and her look or mien nothing of that sweetness or softness feminine which is so ready to captivate, so that it really is a little odd she should have married for love".

Walter, who died in 1792, and Dorothy had two sons, John Strother Ker and Walter Ker. In 1793, two Kelso schoolboys found a bundle in Abbey Close containing a baby who proved to be the illegitimate son of Walter Ker and Agnes Ormiston. The child was named Walter Ker after his father and became a shopkeeper at no. 14 Market Place, selling hardware and jewellery.

Dorothy entered into a contract with John Strother Ker in connection with the ownership of Littledean, but he died in 1795 and his mother survived him for only six years, so by 1802 young Walter had become heir to both. Jeffrey, in his "History of Roxburghshire", mentions a tradition that the last Ker residing at Littledean was killed by a favourite bull which didn't recognise him in his morning-gown. Could this have been the fate of John Strother Ker? It is unlikely to have been Walter as he was better-known in later years as General Ker of Nenthorn.

Walter Ker became a colonel in the Loyal British Fencible Infantry in 1803, a Major-General in 1810 and a Lt.-General by 1814. From 1805 he was heavily involved in his claim to become the 5th Duke of Roxburghe, the 4th Duke having died childless. Walter was heir-male general of Lady Jean Ker, eldest daughter of Harry, son of the first Earl of Roxburghe, and many people regarded his claim as more valid than that of his nearest rival, Sir James Innes. Indeed, so confident was Walter of success, spurred on by his wife's declaration that "she would be a duchess or nothing", that he rejected Sir James' suggestion that the winner should pay all costs, a decision which he lived to regret. When judgement was finally made in favour of Sir James Innes in 1812, Walter Ker was financially ruined.

Walter Ker's maternal grandfather, Alexander Collingwood, died in 1758 and was buried at Whittingham, his pall supported by Lord Ravensworth, Sir Henry Grey, Nicholas Brown, Robert Fenwick, Christopher Reed, Collingwood Forster, Bryan Burrell and Gilbert Park. Alexander's eldest son and namesake, who had married Margaret Brown in 1753, succeeded to the property which presumably was still occupied by his widowed mother and six unmarried sisters. A younger brother, Thomas Collingwood, was in the Royal Navy and perhaps he introduced William Dickson to their sister Jane. At any rate, Jane and William were married in 1765 and the youngest of the Collingwood family, Elizabeth, married John Dickson in 1771.

William and Jane Dickson had three children, including twins, born at Morpeth, but they would appear to have died in infancy. Their next two children, William Dickson and Archibald Collingwood Dickson, were born at Broughton, Peeblesshire, in 1770 and 1772 respectively. They went on to have a daughter, Eleanora (1774), a son, Alexander (1777) and another daughter, Jane (1780). Alexander and Jane were both born at Sydenham, near Kelso. Alexander was baptised by Rev. Richard Wallis, vicar of Carham, who was minister of the Episcopalian Church in Kelso which was attended by the Dickson family and in which they rented a seat.

DICKSON FAMILY TREE - 2nd GENERATION

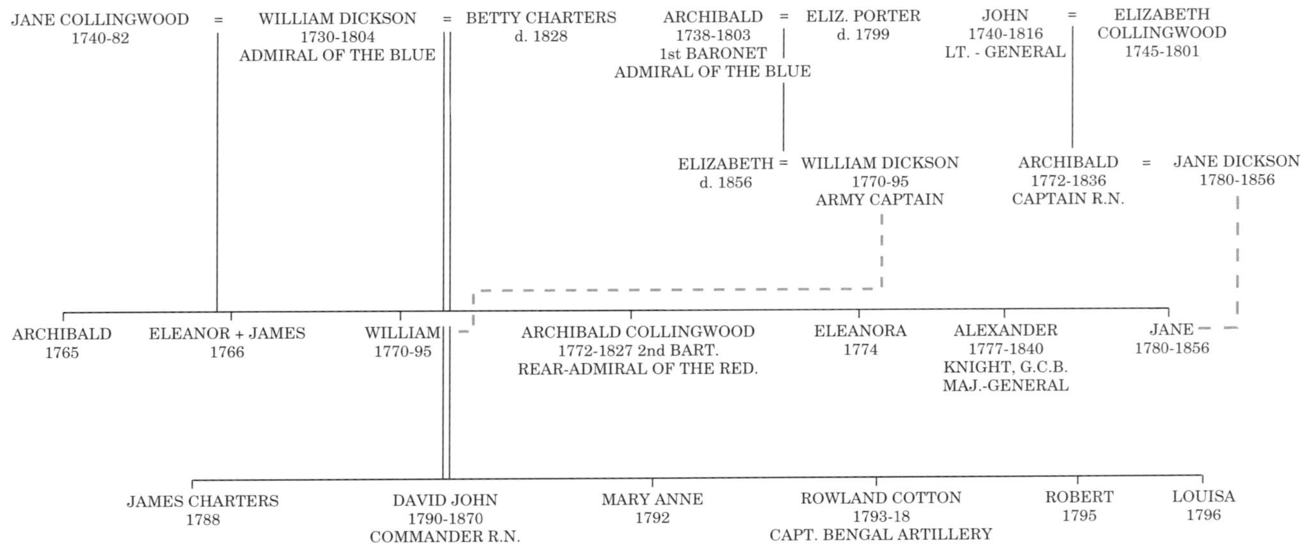

However, Jane was baptised by the Church of Scotland minister of the Parish Church, Rev. Cornelius Lundie. Two years after the birth of her youngest child, Jane Dickson died and left her husband with five children under 12 years of age. It was at this time that William was transferred from the "Sampson" to the "Standard" which was tied up in Plymouth – perhaps the Navy's way of giving him a compassionate posting.

On 19th September 1787, William remarried. His bride was Elizabeth ("Betty") Charters, daughter of James Charters of Eton College, Windsor, and they were married in Kelso by the Rev. Cornelius Lundie. William and Betty stayed on at Sydenham, and in addition to the five children of William's first marriage, they went on to have six children of their own: James Charters (1788); David John (1790); Mary Anne (1792); Rowland Cotton (1793); Robert (1795); and Louisa (1796).

William and Jane's son William joined the army, became a Captain in the 22nd Regiment, and died in 1795, aged 25, at Port-au-Prince, Santo Domingo during the on-going conflict with France and Spain.

Their second surviving son, Archibald Collingwood Dickson, followed in his father's footsteps, joined the Navy and received his first commission as Lieutenant at the age of 19 on the flagship of Sir Alexander Hood. In 1794, Archibald was Lieutenant on the "Royal George" when Lord Howe's action defeated the French fleet, capturing six ships of war. He was next promoted to the Megaera fire-vessel with the rank of Post-Captain. When Admiral William Dickson, his father, succeeded Sir Richard Onslow as a commander in the North Sea fleet, Archibald Collingwood was appointed to his father's flagship the "Monarch" of 74 guns. Five years later he was captain of the "Veteran", 64 guns, which assisted at the capture of the Dutch fleet at Texel and later formed part of the fleet of Sir Hyde Parker when he fought the Northern Confederacy. Archibald's subsequent commands included the "Orion", the "Akbar" and the "Rochfort". He eventually reached the rank of Rear-Admiral of the Red.

Alexander Dickson, third son of Jane and William, also followed a military career. He married Eulalia Briones of Minorca in 1802 and their daughter Jane was born at Sydenham a year later. In 1809 Alexander served under Col. Howarth in Sir Arthur Wellesley (Wellington)'s army in Portugal. He distinguished himself and was invited by Wellington to command the Royal Artillery, comprising 8,000 men and 3-4,000 horses. He was probably the first engineer officer in Europe of his day, becoming Inspector of Artillery in 1822, Major-General in 1838 and A.D.C. to the King. Sir Alexander Dickson died in 1840 at his residence in Charles St., Berkeley Square, London.

William and Betty's son David John joined the Navy, eventually reaching commander, and served under his half-brother, Sir Archibald Collingwood Dickson, on the "Orion" and the "Rochfort". In 1828 he married Hester Rawlins and in 1830 is recorded as living at Croft House, Kelso. He died at Paulton, Bath in 1870.

Rowland Cotton, their second son, became a Captain in the Bengal Artillery and his son, William David, did likewise, being a political agent and judge at Neemuck and a celebrated oriental linguist.

William Dickson made a will in 1801, three years before his death. His eldest surviving son, Archibald Collingwood Dickson, was his heir; Alexander Dickson was to receive £500; their sister Eleanora, presumably unmarried and nearing 30 years of age, was willed £700. Jane, the youngest daughter of William and Jane, married her cousin Archibald, son of John and Elizabeth Dickson, in 1801 and at that time received a marriage portion of £700 which was equivalent to the bequest, so she did not receive a further sum. David John, Rowland Cotton and Robert were still children and were to have £500 each, while their sisters Mary Anne and Louisa would get £700.

Betty Charters, widow of William Dickson, is recorded amongst the Nobility, Gentry and Clergy in Pigot's Directory of Roxburghshire, 1826, living in Kelso at Seven Elms, which is now known as the Elms, Roxburgh Street. (By that time Alexander Ballantyne, who previously occupied the house, had moved across the road to Walton Hall). Betty died in 1828.

Had William, eldest son of William and Jane, lived, he would probably have inherited the title of Baronet from his uncle Archibald, for he had married Sir Archibald's daughter, his cousin Elizabeth. However, as he died in 1795 without issue, his brother Archibald Collingwood Dickson was named as heir apparent and the title descended through that branch of the family. Archibald had married Harriet, daughter of Admiral Bourmaster of Tichfield in Hampshire in 1797 and they had eight of a family. Three of their sons inherited

DICKSON FAMILY TREE - 3rd GENERATION

ARCHIBALD COLLINGWOOD DICKSON
1772-1827
REAR-ADMIRAL OF THE RED
2nd BARONET

=

HARRIET BOURMASTER
d. 1865

HARRIET
d. 1859
m.
ADM. THOS.
CARTER

WILLIAM
1798-1868
VICE-ADMIRAL R.N.
3rd BARONET
m.
LAURA NORTHEY

MARY MAGDALEN
d. 1847
M.
LT.-GEN. CLAUDE
DOUGLAS

JOHN
1804

COLPOYS
1807-1868
COL. BENGAL ARMY
4th BARONET
m.
EMMA KNYVETT

ALEXANDER
COLLINGWOOD THOMAS
1810-1884
CAPTAIN R.N.
5th BARONET
m.
AMELIA WHIMPER

AUGUSTA
d. 1833

JOHN BOURMASTER
1815-1876
REAR-ADMIRAL R.N.
m.
1. SARAH POYNDER
d. 31.10.1866
* JOHN POYNDER
b.31.10.1866
2. ELLEN FRAMPTON

GEORGE
1817-1853
CAPT. ARMY
m.
HENRIETTA
FRAMPTON

FRANCIS
1822
CAPT. ARMY
m.
FRANCES
TURNER

* JOHN POYNDER DICKSON POYNDER
6th BARONET
LATER BARON ISLINGTON
GOVERNOR OF NEW ZEALAND 1910-12

the title in succession but none of them left male heirs. Sir William Dickson, 3rd Baronet, Vice-Admiral, R.N., succeeded his father in 1827 and lived until January 1868. His brother Colpoys, a Lt. Col. in the Bengal Army, only enjoyed his title as 4th Baronet for five months before he too died. The third brother, Alexander Collingwood Thomas Dickson, yet another naval captain, became 5th Baronet in May 1868.

(The Coat of arms below were granted by the College of Heralds in London).

Sir Alexander Collingwood Thomas Dickson

Sir John Poynder Dickson-Poynder

Meanwhile, John Bourmaster Dickson, youngest son of Archibald Collingwood, 2nd Baronet, emulated his father and rose through the naval ranks to become a rear-admiral. At the age of forty he married Sarah Poynder of Hilmarton, Wiltshire in 1855 and they had three daughters. In giving birth to their son, John Poynder, on 31st October, 1866, Sarah died. John Bourmaster re-married two years later but died in 1876. When his brother Alexander, 5th Baronet, died childless in 1884 young John Poynder Dickson succeeded to the title. Ihheriting the Manor of Hilmarton from his uncle Henry Poynder, in 1888 John assumed the additional surname and arms of Poynder, becoming Sir John Poynder Dickson-Poynder, commemorated in Poynder Place, Kelso. Known as "Jack Dickson Poynder", he was friendly with Lord George Scott, brother of the Duke of Buccleuch. The pair studied together for nine months under Captain James for examinations to enter the army, staying at Montagu House. Each morning Sir John would drive them in his phaeton and pair to Lexham Gardens, and later they would walk to their club. Sir John later joined the 3rd Royal Scots and became

A.D.C. to Gen. Lord Methuen during the South African War. From 1892-1910 he was Conservative M.P. for N.W. Wiltshire, and from 1910-12 Governor of New Zealand. He was created Baron Islington on 27th April, 1910.

Islington Coat of Arms

Footnotes:

1) Baronets of Nova Scotia

In 1621, William Alexander, later Earl of Stirling, received a charter from James VI granting him and his heirs part of the Northern section of America, Canada and the islands and giving him permission to exercise absolute authority. After the accession of Charles I in 1625, the charter and rights were renewed, and the Castlehill in Edinburgh was held to be the soil of Nova Scotia. The first batch of Baronets of Nova Scotia was created entitling them, on payment of £150 sterling, to a grant of land 3 miles long by 2 miles broad. From 1625 to 1649, sixty-four baronets took seisen of the soil of Castlehill.

2) Scots Currency *was supposed to have been abolished at the Act of Union in 1707, but obviously took some time to disappear from use. A pound Scots was equivalent to 1s. 8d. sterling; a Scots penny was a twelfth the value of 1d sterling.*

3) Squadron Colours

Squadron Colours were said to have been inaugurated in the time of Queen Elizabeth of England.

Admiral – red flag; Vice-Admiral – white flag; Rear-Admiral – blue flag; a Rear-Admiral of the Blue became a Rear-Admiral of the White as a first step; a Rear-Admiral of the Red became a Vice-Admiral of the Blue. There was no Admiral of the Red, as he was in overall charge of the whole fleet.

At the time of Trafalgar, the rank of Admiral of the Red was introduced as Admiral of the Fleet and the rank was held for life.

This system was discontinued in 1864, when the Red Ensign denoted the Mechant Navy, the White Ensign the Royal Navy and the Blue Ensign the Auxiliary fleet.

CHAPTER ONE – SOURCES

Mediaeval Towns – Edinburgh by Oliver Smeaton

Foster's Baronetage 1882

The Baron Court of Stichill – Gunn

The Records of the Pringles – Alexander Pringle

Memoirs of Walter Pringle

History of Roxburghshire – Jeffrey

History of Peeblesshire – Chambers

Whittingham Vale – David Dippie Dixon

Ridpath's Diary – Rev. George Ridpath

Ednam and its Indwellers – Burleigh

Border Memories – W.R. Carre

Kelso Past & Present – Vernon

Rutherfurd's Southern Counties Register

Kelso Old Parish Register

Stichill Old Parish Register

International Genealogical Index

Dictionary of National Biography

Admiralty papers held at Greenwich

Admiralty Records held at Public Records Office, Kew.

Scottish Records Office

A System of Heraldry – Nisbet

Burke's General Armory

Rear Admirals of the White

Biographia Navalis – Charnock

The Fleeting Opportunity – Lord George Scott

Life of Sir Walter Scott – Lochhart

CHAPTER TWO

FORTUNE

When James Dickson went to school at Stichill, the schoolmaster was Andrew Whale, whose son Lancelot was to become headmaster of Kelso Grammar School in 1780. The standard of education in Scotland at that time was very high, and young men with a Scottish education were much in demand in London. James arrived in that city at a time when the economy was rapidly expanding, partly fostered by the constant need for supplies and victuals for ships attending the various arenas of war in Europe and beyond. According to Jeffrey, in his "History of Roxburghshire", Dickson "amassed a considerable fortune by purchasing, while a navy agent, shares due to the capture of the Havannah". This event happened in 1762, but James Dickson was apparently already a wealthy man, for in January 1760, George Ridpath, minister of Stichill, noted in his diary that £5, to be distributed among the poor, had been received from "one Dickson, a native of this parish, and now a merchant in London, where he is grown very rich, sent down to Smith of Jedburgh, who is a relation of his."

There does not seem to be any remaining record of James Dickson's life as a merchant, but a study of prevailing practices and sources of income gives an idea of his general activities. His marriage to Betty Hogg is recorded as having taken place at St. Katherine-by-the-Tower in 1739, but his name doesn't appear on the list of merchants until 1754, when his address is given as the Crutched Friars, corner of Gold Square. The Crutched Friars still exists, a narrow street near the Tower of London, no doubt a good deal altered; Gold Square disappeared during the development of the railway track and station at Fenchurch Street. Crutched Friars was mainly inhabited by merchants, many of whom had names denoting Scottish origin, such as Buchanan, Scott, Hogg (possibly Betty's family?), Bell, Douglas and Smale. James Dickson is also recorded as having a glass warehouse in Blackfriars, which later was transferred to Fleet Street. His friend, Albert Innes, whose name appears as witness on several documents, also had an address at Gold Square.

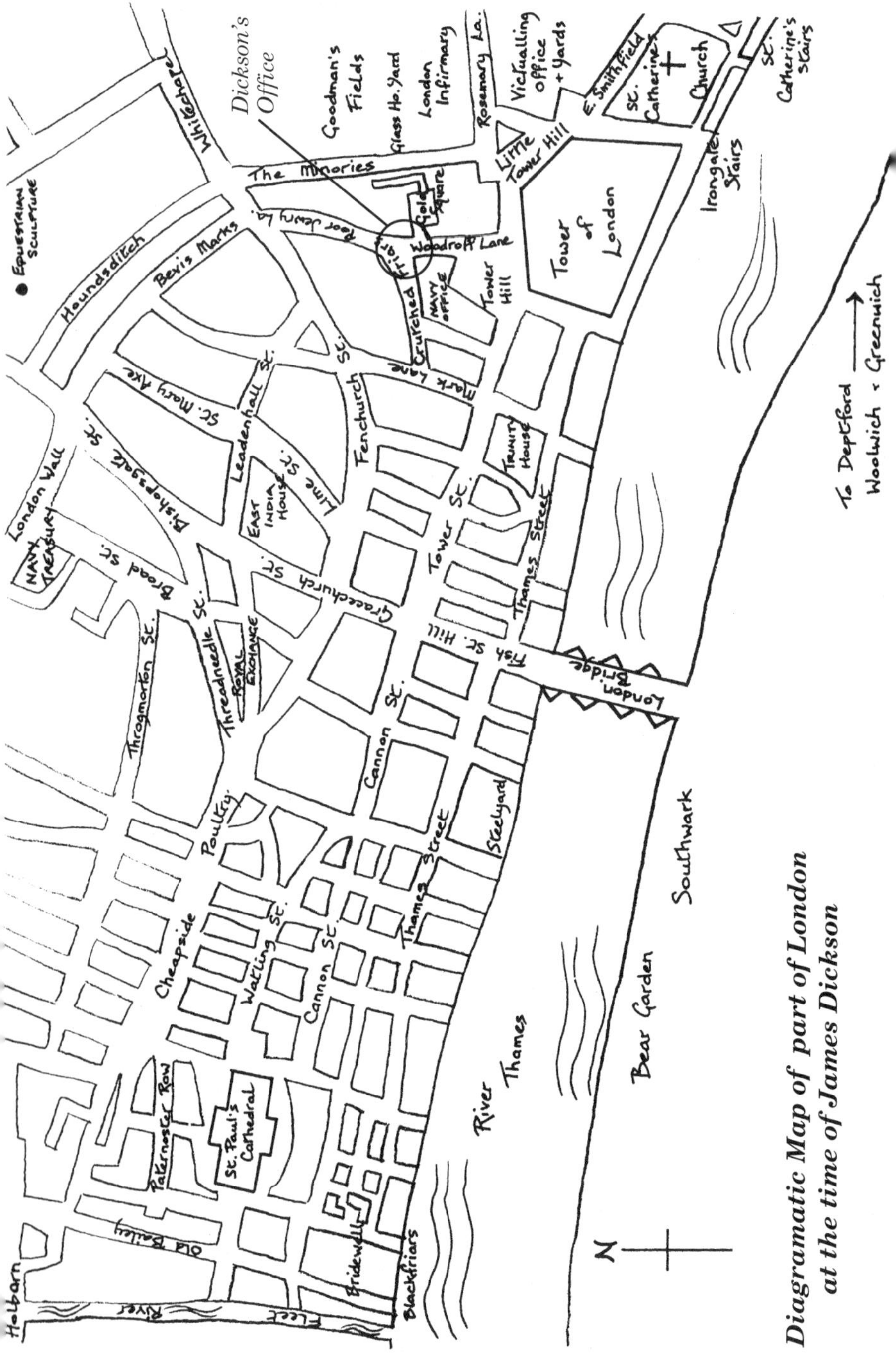

Diagramatic Map of part of London at the time of James Dickson

The area of London adjacent to the Tower was of great antiquity. Dark, narrow alleyways were full of ruinous old houses, occupied by people taking in lodgers at 2d per night, with four or five beds in a room, while the cellars or garrets might be let to whole families. There was considerable stench and risk to health from the lack of sanitation and the death-rate was appallingly high, necessitating immigration to renew the population. In many cases, ownership of property was uncertain or on short lease, so there was no incentive to renovate. Some new building was done, but the bricks were often made on the spot, using earth from the foundations, and beams were made of thin wood, so the results were somewhat ramshackle. These conditions contrasted markedly with the fine new streets and Squares which were under construction elsewhere, particularly in West London, so wealthy merchants chose to live some distance from their place of business.

At that time, one of the most profitable trades was distilling, which gave farmers a market for cereals at a time of low prices; landowners a vested interest in rents for land; and shipowners business in transporting produce. Employers sold gin to their workpeople and "Geneva shops" multiplied all over the city, leading to drunkenness, misery and violence. Children, neglected or deserted by intoxicated parents, ended up in workhouses or wandering the streets, undernourished and diseased. There was an epidemic of fever in 1741, with incredible mortality due to poverty, overcrowding and dirt, partly as a result of alcoholism, so an Act to reduce the consumption of spirits was passed in 1743, followed by a more rigourous sequel in 1751, and gradually the situation improved.

By degrees, the ruinous houses in the vicinity of the Tower were replaced by warehouses and counting-houses where employment was given to agents, factors, insurers, bankers, brokers and other dealers in money. This was the area where Samuel Pepys, as a naval administrator about 70 years previously, lived and conducted his business from Seething Lane, where the Navy Office was situated. That had been the period of the Restoration of Charles II; now the King was George II, Pitt was prime minister, and Britain was at war with the French over the colonies in North America. Samuel Pepys had improved the efficiency of naval administration, but in 1715 there was still disorder and accounts were overdue, so the Victualling Board took over in an attempt to straighten out the chaos.

There were agents at various out-ports who had large sums of cash at their disposal, by bills of exchange or Treasury imprests for which they were accountable. In 1740, agents were assigned to the West Indies and given large imprests for buying provisions locally or in North America, but unfortunately defrauded the Navy of £50,000. The facilities for the outports were developed and improved, with storehouses, bakehouses, cooperages, wharves and breweries being built.

At Deptford, on the Thames, there had long been a dockyard and in 1742 an adjacent estate called Redhouse was purchased from Sir John Evelyn to extend the naval base and relieve the congestion at Tower wharf. There were already storehouses and a long wharf there, which had been used by the Transport Office for the English cavalry travelling to Flanders. Transport of goods around the wharves was carried out by carmen, those having the necessary licence recognisable by the brass plate on the shafts of the cart, with a number and the City Arms branded on them; carmen operating illegally were fined 10/- for every offence. It was also against the law to use more than one horse to a cart, except uphill, or when it was impossible to divide the load; the penalty was 10/- for a first offence, 20/- for the second, and so on, the extra horse being impounded until the fine was paid. Those waiting to work on the wharves, doing tackle or crane-work, had to stand in order and take their turn, but a merchant requiring a cart for other purposes could select whichever he pleased.

One of the anomolies to be tackled was the practice of delivering water to the ships, instead of having the ship's boat pick it up. Ships required an endless supply of goods of bewildering variety, as most of them expected to be at sea for months at a time and even the stores at the outports had to be stocked with goods which were shipped to them from the home base. Although the Navy seemed to be constantly preparing for war against one enemy or another, there were other reasons for going to sea. In a letter to the Navy Office in March 1769, Captain Charles Douglas writes from his ship the "Emerald":

> *"...ordered to the North Cape of Lapland where the transit of Venus is to be observed...engaged John Saunders as pilot...he has a qualification from Trinity House for the whole of the North Sea. The ship is to be victualled for 5 months....beer for one month, spirits for the rest. The present Brandy Room is*

not sufficient to contain the quantity of spirits ....to order the builder at Sheerness to enlarge it....need medicine for the sick and wounded and apparatus for viewing the transit of Venus. Mr Anderson Surgeon's 2nd mate has been left sick at Leith, continuing so ill that he is unable to return to duty...recommend Robert White instead."

Another letter sent from Barbados by Commander Charles Knowles to the Admiralty in October 1746 illustrates the difficulty in recruiting and keeping crews:

"...so soon as they can get manned, the privateers having taken away most of their men, and the rest secreted ashore for adventurers for others. Merchants will have as great reason to complain for privateers not only invagle their men but take 'em by force and beat the masters and mates if they don't deliver their chests and bedding."

Privateer crews at that time were unpaid and relied on prize money, so that the motivation for capturing ships was a powerful one. "Letters of marque" allowed merchantmen to take advantage of any chance capture and keep the profits. The Royal Navy was a better prospect, as the wages were good and the possibilty of prize-money and advancement were attractive inducements for poor or ill-educated young men. By 1760, the Royal Navy had expanded from 10,000 to 85,000 men within 5 years, while the merchant service declined from 34,000 to 20,000. Press-gangs helped to swell the numbers and although this was unpopular, it was seen as essential, and preferable to conscription. Debtors of under £20 were released from prison if they would join up, and men from other countries sometimes chose the British Navy rather than become prisoners of war. Volunteers joining the Navy in wartime could expect a bounty offered by proclamation and to receive two months wages in advance - in 1759 this amounted to £7 for an able-seaman. Sometimes slaves were forced into service, but the Navy disapproved as it was opposed to slavery. In London, the Marine Society took poor boys off the street, gave them clothes and some training, and sent them to sea. Landlords had been known to draft their tenants, particularly their own countrymen. Unlike the army, officers did not require wealth to obtain their commissions. Many joined up as boys and were trained free, sometimes as servants to officers, to gain experience and serve their time. From petty officer they could reach lieutenant in a few years. Even unwarlike seamen such as pursers, who were not expected to expose themselves to danger during action, could win promotion by gallantry. The purser's main chance of wealth and success lay in private business, in broking, moneylending and as agent. He was responsible for victuals issued by the Victualling Board and accountable for the entire value of the stores provided, keeping detailed and complex paperwork on all aspects. As he was responsible for casks, he worked closely with the ship's cooper. He was expected to supply, at his own expense, consumable stores such as coal and firewood for galleys, oil and candles; he issued clothing from the Navy Board and provided tobacco as a private enterprise. A purser spent out large sums in the hope of eventual return, with profit, but if a ship was lost and his books and papers went with it, he could be ruined. He often acted as banker for officers who had to wait for their pay, as they could not draw their cash until the ship was paid off at the end of her commission. All those, perhaps half the crew, who were discharged before that time received only a ticket for their wages, which they could cash on pay-off day. There was a flourishing trade in buying tickets at discount, often by pursers, but the broker might be an inn-keeper or a merchant, who would get 5/- or 6/- in the pound. Seamen, who paid 6d a month towards Greenwich Hospital, might be receiving treatment there when the ship was paid off and have to wait years before they even received a ticket. The families of seamen were often impoverished by this practice of discount and delay, but after the regulations were tightened in 1758, ticket-broking declined and a seaman could appear in person and demand his wages. Ships usually paid out just before they sailed, lying out from shore, as men very often deserted when they had money in their pockets.

Frigate of c.1752

Prize money was acceptable as a reward for patriotism and was divided out among the crew according to rank: 8-12 shares to officers, 1-2 shares to able seaman, $1/4$ – 1 share to boys. On privateers, owners took $1/2$ any prize money, whereas warships divided the entire prize among the captors. Obviously, the smaller the ship, the less opportunity it had to capture large and well-armed ships, so successful ships were larger and had a greater number of crew to share the prize-money. Officers, particularly the higher ranks, could make a great deal of money and many dreamt of buying estates with the proceeds on their return home. A prize agent had to have power of attorney signed by a majority of the ship's company before the Navy Office would allow him to pass the captors' accounts. A squadron might appoint one agent for all the ships; the agency was so valuable it was often given to a follower of the captain, and the most successful agents were those whose captains became admirals. On rare occasions, the zeal for prize-money could lead to dereliction of duty by disobeying orders in pursuit of a potential captive.

Another major operational field for ships and market for suppliers was the West Indies sugar trade, which had been established in the 17th century. In fact, commerce was as much a reason for continual conflict with Spain and France as the political will to conquer and expand territory. Coin money was in short supply and barter was unacceptable because of the fluctuation in the price of sugar, so Spanish coin was often used in the trade, which caused problems in time of war. In 1739, when Britain went to war with Spain, ostensibly over alleged barbarities of the Spanish coast-guards in suppressing illicit trade, one of the main reasons was the interrupted supply of coin, the other to force large concessions for trade with Spanish America. The capture of Porto Bello during that war increased the circulation of Spanish money, thus enriching Jamaica. France, Spain and Portugal all had their plantations on various West Indian islands, many of them run more efficiently than the British and therefore able to undercut the price of exported sugar.

Inextricably linked with this was the slave trade, which was accepted in those days without scruple. Native populations were often the victims of tribal warfare and slave-dealers were as likely to be from among their own people as to be traders from other nations. In 1739, 95 ships left England for Africa and transported 3,008 black people to Jamaica. In 1743, 71 ships transported 8,540, rising four years later to 10,898 on board only 68 ships, indicating serious overcrowding and

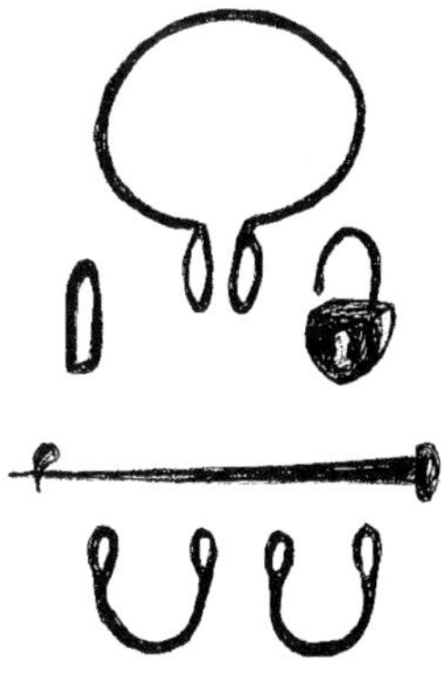

Iron collar and fetters used by slavers

the accompanying risk of disease. Captains did not willingly go all the way to Jamaica if they could possibly stop at the Windward Islands, as the extra distance increased the risk of capture, or of suicide or revolt among the "cargo". The price of an able slave in 1749 was £9 or £10 on the Gold Coast, fetching £29 or £30 in the West Indies.

These ships had to be insured, but this posed difficulties as the insurers, particularly at a distance, could not satisfy themselves that the vessels were sea-worthy. For this reason, London underwriters charged more than those in Philidelphia or Boston. In 1744, London insurers underwrote a ship bound for Barbados at 15 guineas, to "return 7 guineas if she chanced to take convoy for the whole voyage". The Royal African Company was the original transporter of slaves, but their high prices led to independent traders setting up in London, Bristol or Liverpool. They were in competition with others from America, France, Holland, Portugal and Denmark, and at times there was international trade where the Dutch or French would sell their slaves to the British, either for money or a commodity such as indigo. The South Sea Company set up factories in Jamaica and imported slaves to transport them on to the Spanish colonies; the Spanish had a factory at Havannah, Cuba and 30 new sugar-works.

The sugar planters tended to be the wealthy members of society since it required vast amounts of money to set up a plantation, and their social and political values tended to be those of the rural aristocracy. Those planters who were resident took pride in their island and its government, but were too busy amassing fortunes to take an interest in defence or expansion, preferring to leave that to the armed forces. In 1702, Admiral Benbow remarked on this and complained that he could "hardly get provisions to support the sick, the ships and the soldiers being a great burden to them and wish they had never come". In the main, their children were sent home to be educated, often refusing to return; those who remained were spoiled. Most planters, however, regarded the West Indies as a temporary business and preferred to remain at home in their own elegant, well-furnished country houses. This absence of proprietors led to mismanagement of the plantations, the agents and overseers being careless or extravagent, or their cruelty leading to insurrection by the slaves. Absentee planters would hold meetings in taverns and coffee-houses in London, charging their expenses to the colony.

Because vast tracts of land were owned by one planter, small settlers were deterred and cultivation was less than it should have been. When, in 1735, merchants in various ports pointed this out to the King, attempts at reform were introduced in the form of grants and inducements. However, the settlers were often ejected by the big landowners after they had purchased slaves and cleared and planted the land, with loss of capital, so the scheme was abandoned. The price of sugar from British colonies was double that on the Continent, so merchants petitioned to be allowed to import sugar from abroad, but the bill going through Parliament was smothered by the strong planting interest among members. There were complaints about the monopoly in the sugar trade and the taxes imposed by a cartel amongst the planters. At the same time, there was resentment that those who were becoming wealthy estate owners as a result should be able to contest parliamentary seats in the richest and most populous cities in the country. People were unable to afford British refined sugar and bought brown instead, so the home-based refineries suffered. As refined sugar took up less room than raw sugar, permitting the colonies to use slave labour to refine their own sugar would reduce the number of transport ships needed.

Very often, sea captains were financially involved with the sugar trade, perhaps as planters, or with other commodities from the West Indies such as rum, ginger, cotton, indigo or cocoa and were therefore anxious that homeward-bound convoys should be protected. Naval officers could also be members of Parliament and some seats were actually in the control of the Admiralty. At one stage, in 1761, Lord Anson controlled 15 members, the largest faction in the House of Commons, mainly admirals, who were expected to support the ministry with their votes on all important matters. They had direct control of Dartmouth, Plymouth, Portsmouth, Rochester, Saltash and Sandwich and shared Queenborough with the Ordnance Board.

Captain James Douglas, of Springwood Park in Kelso, was M.P. for St. Ola in Orkney, 1754-68, in the Earl of Morton's interest, and raised men there. Born in 1704, the son of George Douglas of Friarshaw and his wife Elizabeth Scott of Ancrum, James joined the Navy, patronised by Pulteney, and received his first commission in 1734. He bought Bridgend Park in Kelso in 1750 from Sir William Ker of Greenhead, renamed it Springwood and rebuilt the house. James Douglas received his knighthood and £500 in 1759, when, serving under Sir Charles Saunders, he was chosen to bring home the despatch following Wolfe's capture of Quebec from the French.

The capture of Guadaloupe by Britain the same year gained the richest colony in the Americas, but it added to the duties of the Royal Navy in protecting coastal trade from the French privateers, mostly sloops and schooners, whose base was in Martinique. The West Indies was the only place where vessels, suitable to counter the French, could be bought privately. Sir James Douglas owned two in succession; one – a sloop – called "Experiment" was captured by the French. Douglas wrote to his agent, George Poplay, at Jamaica in 1762:

> *"The sloop "Experiment" belonging to me in the King's service was taken by a French privateer while en route express to Geo. Pocock. You demand payment of storekeeper Mr. Paterson at Port Royal for same; she was valued at £1,000. There were 5 negroes in her – my own loss".*

In 1760, Sir James was ordered to hoist a broad pendant as a Commodore with a captain under him, to relieve Commodore Moore as Commander-in-Chief in the Leeward Islands. He began to send French prisoners, captured privateersmen, to England but this proved counter-productive as the French retaliated in kind and the squadron, which relied on manning ships with returned prisoners, suffered. He also tended to use slaves, some of whom had been made prisoners of war, to man his private sloops, but this was frowned upon by the Navy. A letter from Antigua that year notes:

> *"William Barkham has drawn by Commander in Chief Sir James Douglas 21 setts of bills value £4,000 to defray expenses – stores purchased etc."*

On the back of this letter are scribbled the cautionary words

> *"not enough information being given".*

The Seven Years War, which began in 1756, involved Britain and Prussia as allies against France, Austria and Russia, with Sweden joining at a later date to exclude foreign vessels from the Baltic. The Royal Navy was increasingly involved as the war progressed and Sir James Douglas, by then a post-captain with 12 years seniority, made preparations for the capture of the French base at Martinique. Admiral Rodney, apparently in jealousy, moved swiftly against Martinique without acknowledging Douglas' help.

Rodney then sent Douglas unverified orders under his secretary's hand and when Douglas tactfully rebuked him, Rodney insisted on taking all Douglas' best ships, including the flagship and most of the frigates. Meanwhile, there were plans afoot for a much bigger expedition and Rodney was ordered to abandon the siege of Martinique and to hold his forces in readiness.

The British public hoped that appropriation of more West Indian islands would ease the monopoly held by the sugar planters. Indeed, there was a "Scheme for the taking of Santo Domingo" as this island produced nearly as much sugar as all the British islands put together. Trade between Santo Domingo and North America could expand the British market. In 1762, Spain was forced to enter the war as an ally of France, although Portugal sided with the British. The centre of Spanish power in the Caribbean was at "the Havannah", Cuba. It had an excellent naval base in a good harbour, and the fort of El Morro, which overlooked the entrance, was regarded as impregnable by the Spanish. Not only did the base command communications between Spain and her American colonies, but it was reputed to be rich in booty. The loss of Havannah would deal a severe blow to Spanish power in America and the British decided to capture it. In order to disguise their real intent, the main British force would threaten several places en route – Puerto Rico, Hispaniola and Santo Domingo, proceeding along the northern shore of Cuba to Havannah. Preparations were on an enormous scale and the plan was to leave in mid-February, but this was delayed due to a shortage of bedding. Reading some of the letters from storekeepers a few years prior, the suspicion grows that the plan had been simmering for some time before the declaration of war. In January, 1757, Mr. Greenway, store-keeper at Portsmouth Dock says he has 66 beds in store and 820 due. He asks the Navy Board to

> *"hasten them hither – I fear some disappointment will happen to the service for want of them".*

And in April:

> *"200 hammocks lately received by land carriage. The "William and Charlotte" not yet arrived with a further supply. Wind still unfair – many hammocks now wanting for the ships under orders for the Foreign Service. 1,000 wanted immediately for "Invincible" and others".*

In January, 1762, the Admiralty directed the Navy Board to provide 10,000 tons of transports for overseas service at Spithead, where there were already 3 transports and 32 ships just arrived from Belle-Isle needed time to unload and refit. The Ordnance and Victualling Boards assembled ships in the Thames – 2,500 tons of ordnance ships to carry engineers, artillery men and ordnance stores; 16,000 tons of victuallers to convey 7 months army rations for 16,000 men. The expedition eventually got under way in March 1762 and one of the first to arrive in the West Indies was Sir James Douglas in the "Dublin". His main objective, despite Rodney's orders, was to rendezvous with Sir George Pocock, gaining superiority over French and Spanish squadrons, and this he finally achieved in May. When Pocock and his fleet did arrive off Havannah, the Governor of Cuba and other Spanish officials were in church, celebrating the feast of Trinity. Being unaware that they were at war with Britain, the Cubans thought it was a friendly visit – until they saw troops preparing to land. A boom was thrown across the harbour entrance and the garrison had 5-10,000 troops, while there were ships and seamen in the harbour, so the Spanish were confident of holding out. The worst threat came from disease, for there was yellow fever in Havannah and the British troops, under Albemarle and Maj.-Gen. George Elliot, were suffering from diseases acquired in Martinique. There was no time to lose, so while Pocock staged a diversion at Chorera, the British infantry embarked in flat-bottomed boats and began to advance along the beach. The Spaniards were bombarded from the sea and retreated in confusion, abandoning their fortifications, and chaos reigned. These exercises were repeated and the Spanish hoped desperately to prolong the battle until the hurricanes came or until tropical diseases overcame the British. After a siege lasting until August, American provincial troops and British regular reinforcements arrived from New York, and the fort of El Morro surrendered. The batteries opened fire and the Spanish realised it was only a matter of time before the city was stormed: there was a truce while terms were agreed before capitulation. The British occupied Havannah for 10 months, until the peace of Paris which ended the Seven Years War. The prize money from this rich capture was £737,000 – an enormous sum, the bulk of it going to the two commanders, Pocock and Albemarle, in 1772. Sir James Douglas unsuccessfully demanded a share, and only received the same as the other 41 captains – £4,821.The rest was apportioned according to rank, the 12,607 able seamen getting £10 each.

Despite the wealth amassed by the commanders and their forces in this exercise, 800 seamen amd 500 marines had lost their lives, mainly through disease, which had also killed 4,708 troops. Havannah was returned to Spain in exchange for the Floridas and Britain gained Grenada, Tobago, St. Vincent and Dominica. Sir James Douglas returned to Scotland, a disappointed man. In his mansion at Springwood he hung a large picture by Swain, showing the Spanish ships lying at anchor in the harbour during the siege of Havannah. He was eventually rewarded with a baronetcy in 1786, the year before he died.

Springwood House

There is no doubt that Sir James Douglas was well-known to James Dickson, for he was named as a trustee in Dickson's will. His estate at Springwood Park in Kelso was on the southern bank of the river Tweed, in full view of Dickson's small mansion-house, and the two properties were at either end of the ill-fated stone-arch bridge which was built over a period of three years from 1756- 1759. Both men and their families attended St. Andrew's Episcopal Church, Sir James joining the congregation in 1765.

The town of Kelso at this time was small, but growing, with a population of around 3,000. The main focus now centred on Easter Kelso, the grounds of Floors Castle having extended to encompass the former site of Wester Kelso, which had been replaced by an orchard within the castle wall. The Market Place with the Town House was much the same shape as it is today, with the streets of

Horsemarket and Woodmarket heading eastward, and the High Street, formerly the Common Way and now Roxburgh Street, running from the gates of Floors Castle, across the square and continuing down towards the bridge at the southern end of town. Small wynds led from the main streets, mostly leading to the river bank, and these were full of thatched dwellings, some of them still ruinous from the end of the seventeenth century.

James Dickson returned to his native soil around 1760, rich beyond the dreams of most Kelsonians, and began to buy extensively, both in the town and the surrounding countryside. His transactions occupy 16 pages in the register of Sasines, naming people and boundaries which have long since disappeared. He spread his net wide, buying pieces of land adjoining, but belonging to different owners, from the edge of Kelso eastwards, towards Ednam. There was a natural boundary known as Blackmuir Dyke, in the Broomlands area, and another was formed by Eden Water; there was a plantation called Angraflat, and common ground at Lillie Loch; the fields of Bernington have been lost to memory, while the lands of Spittle recalled a mediaeval hospital known as St. Leonard's. The list of proprietors includes some familiar surnames: – Jamieson, Miller, Armstrong, Ancrum, Ormston, Waldie, Stewart, Chatto, the names recurring in connection with properties in the town of Kelso itself.

James Dickson bought lands in the town which now include Poynder Park and Place, the ground on which Kelso Hospital stands, and Forestfield, which later became nursery ground. He bought numerous properties on the bank of the Tweed, from Oven Wynd, along Bridge Street to Abbey Close. Tenements of land there were known as "the Almery", one of which was possessed by Thomas Davidson, surgeon before it was purchased by Dickson. In 1787, this tenement was sold by Captain William Dickson to Alexander Mein, skinner. Mason, in his "Kelso Records" states that all houses are held in feu from the Duke except David Mein's house, which is held direct from the crown under tenure of presenting a white rose to the king whenever he enters Kelso. (Is there a connection and a story here?)

The registration of all Dickson's acquisitions in Kelso finishes in the usual legal fashion of the day, with the Duke of Roxburghe appending his signature as Superior:

"In witness whereof these presents and each page thereof consisting of this and the twentysix preceeding pages written on stamped vellum by Patrick Panton, writer to William Ker my Clerk & Chamberlain and I have caused my proper seal to be hereunto appended. At London the twelfth day of June one thousand seven hundred and sixtysix years before these witnesses – Robert Smith Esq. and Thomas Reidish my servitor (signed) Roxburghe".

John Smith was acting for James Dickson as Attorney in this instance, and the witnesses in Kelso were James Hardie and Thomas Walker, merchants and feuars.

James Dickson used the services of John Waldie, writer in Kelso, when he drew up his will in 1767 and the deed of entail the following year, but when he previously purchased the estate at Broughton in Peeblesshire in 1764, his lawyer was Walter Scott. Walter (1729-1799) was the eldest son of Robert Scott of Sandyknowe, a farm near Kelso, and related to the Scotts of Harden. After an apprenticeship with George Chalmers, W.S., Walter had set up his own practice in Edinburgh. His son, Sir Walter Scott, says of his father: "Most attorneys have been suspected, more or less justly, of making their own fortune at the expense of their clients – my father's fate was to vindicate his calling from the stain in one instance, for in many cases his clients contrived to ease him of considerable sums. Many worshipful and be-knighted names occur to my memory, who did him the honour to run in his debt to the amount of thousands, and to pay him with a lawsuit, or a commission of bankruptcy, as the case happened." As Robert Scott, older brother of Sir Walter, was "bred in the King's service" under Captain William Dickson, nephew and heir to James, it is to be hoped that the relationship between attorney and client in this case was an amicable one.

Walter Scott, W.S.

Appendix 1
Ships participating in the Siege of Havannah

Warships:
Actaeon, Aeolus, Alarm, Alcide, Amazon, Antigua, Aquilon, Arrogant, Aventure, Barbados, Basilisk, Belleisle, Boreas, Bonetta, Burford, Cambridge, Centaur, Centurion, Cerberus, Chesterfield, Crescent, Culloden, Cygnet, Danae, Defiance, Deptford, Devonshire, Dover, Dragon, Dublin, Echo, Edgar, Enterprise, Falkland, Ferret, Fly, Fowey, Glasgow, Grenado, Guadeloupe, Hampshire, Hampton Court, Hussar, Infante, Intrepid, Lizard, Lurcher, Marlborough, Mercury, Namur, Norwich, Nottingham, Orford, Pembroke, Penzance, Porcupine, Port Mahon, Port Royal, Richmond, Ripon, Rochester, Rose, St. Florentine, Sardine, Stirling Castle, Sutherland, Temeraire, Temple, Thunder, Trent, Valiant, Vanguard, Viper, Virgin, Woolwich, Yarmouth, Zephyr.

Spanish Ships:
Colorado, Concepcion, Pastora, St. Joseph, Grande Padre de Dios, Asuncion, Africe, Aguila, America, Aquilon, Arrogante, Asia, Castilla, Conquistador, Dichoso, Europa, Firme, Flecha, Flora, Galicana, Infante, Marte, Monarca, Neptuno, Pallas, Perla, Phoenix, Rema, San Antonio, San Jenaro, Serio, Soberano, Thetis, Tigre, Tridente, Vencedor, Venganza.

Names and Positions of Spanish Ships in the painting by Swain, "The Taking of the Havannah", which used to hang in Springwood House

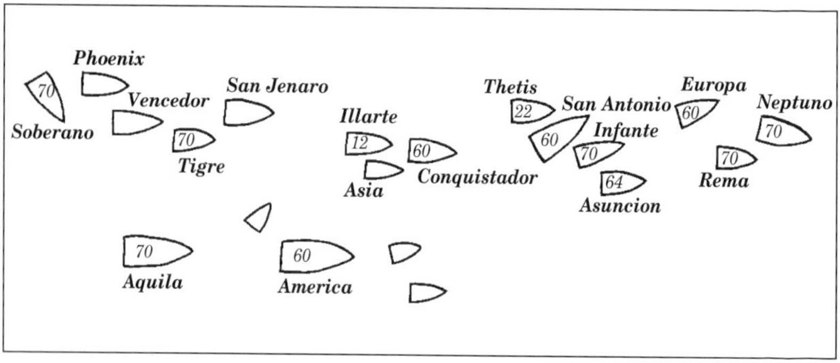

78 British Warships, 37 Spanish Warships

CHAPTER TWO - SOURCES

The Siege and Capture of Havanah – David Syrett

The Douglas Papers – N.A.M. Rodger

London Life in the 18th Century – Dorothy George

Admiralty papers held at Greenwich and Kew

War & Trade in the West Indies – Richard Pares

The Development of the British West Indies – Pitman

Naval Administration 1715-50 – Daniel A. Baugh

Life of Sir Walter Scott – Lockhart

Records held at Scottish Record Office

The Shorter Pepys – Robert Latham

The Wooden World – N.A.M. Rodger

Records of St. Andrew's Church, Kelso

Kelso Records – Mason

History of Roxburghshire – Jeffrey

Title deeds from the Register of Sasines

Plan of Lodging House belonging to Ker of Chatto in Kelso (now site of Ednam House)

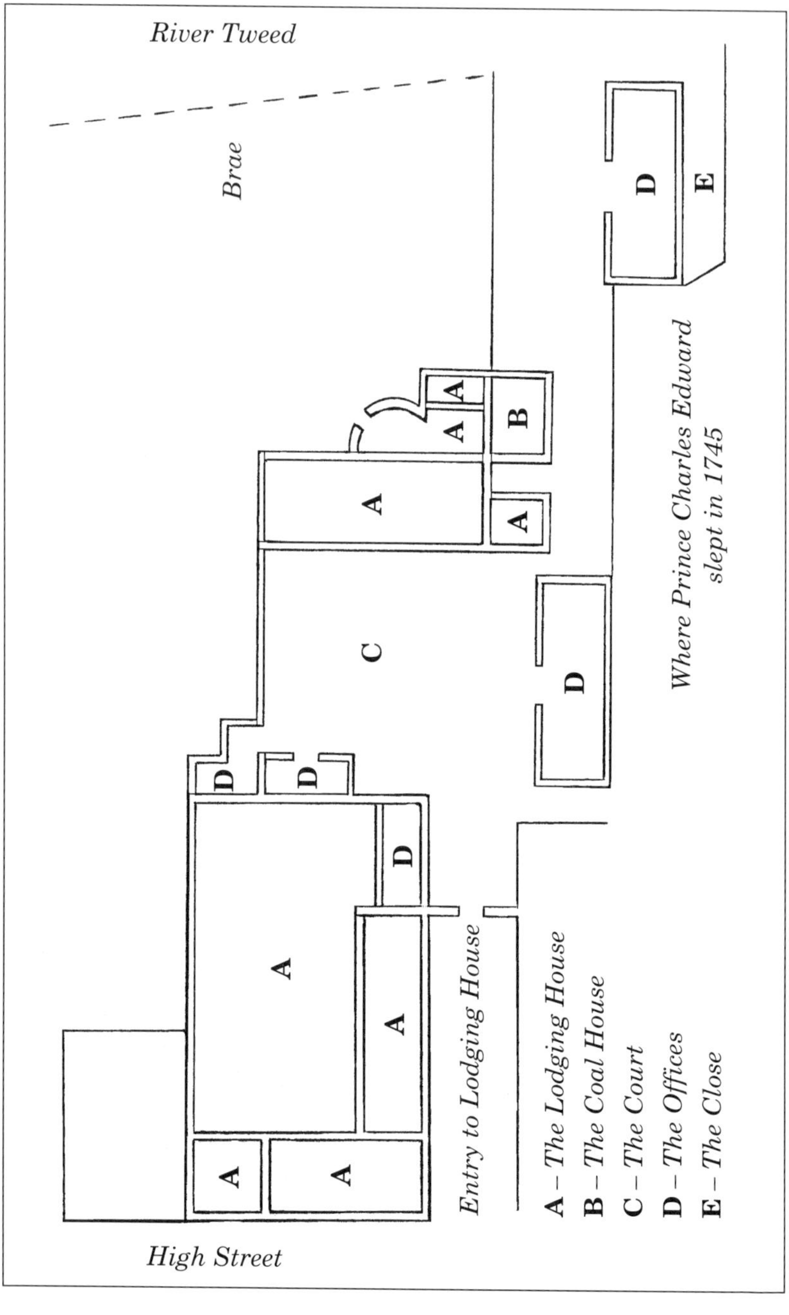

CHAPTER THREE

EDNAM HOUSE

On the banks of the Tweed at Kelso, adjacent to the old mill which had been operated by the monks of Kelso Abbey, was an area set back from the line of houses in the High Street, now known as Bridge Street. On the map of 1684, this area was marked "Laird of Chatto" – at that time William Ker of Chatto – and was inherited by John Ker of Frogden. It consisted of a collection of tenements of land, yards and dwellings known as "Almery Land", thought to be a derivation of "Almoner's Land", probably connected to the Abbey. The house which stood there had once belonged to Ker of Broomlands and then to the Earl of Roxburghe, who passed it on to his son Henry before it was sold to Ker of Chatto. At the time when James Dickson returned to Kelso the house was known as the Chatto Lodging House and had been used by Bonnie Prince Charlie on his visit to Kelso in 1745. To the east, fronting the High Street, stood the small mansion of Charles Ormiston (in recent years best known as Stempel's Tea Rooms). Adjacent, to the south, was the "Court Yett" which formed a gap in the row of houses and prevented the fire of 1684 from spreading further. Beside it stood a tenement and yard once belonging to John Lermont and sold by Elizabeth Lermont to John Ker of Frogden. Excluded from the sale was a piece of waste ground on the east side of the wall, sold by Alexander Scott of Thirlston and Walter Scott of Harden to the Duke of Roxburghe who in 1738 built a weigh-house on this site. At the foot of Oven Wynd was an onstead, or tenement with yard, belonging to Robert Ker, which had once been a Work-house. These properties, together with various tenements in the vicinity, the ownership complex to relate, were purchased by James Dickson during the 1760s and demolished to form one large site on which to build his mansion house.

A tenement "sometime pertaining to William Buncle and then James Hardie, now erected into a chappel for service of the Church of England" stood in Abbey Close. St. Andrew's was opened for public worship on the first of January, 1764, when Rev. Richard Wallis led a service of consecration. Prior to this, Episcopalians had been suppressed by the Hanoverian monarchy for fear they might favour the Stuarts, and clergy were obliged to swear allegiance to King George III. From 1757 onwards, the congregation in Kelso held services in a meeting-room in Woodmarket, with the clergyman communicating from the next room, through a hole in the wall. James Dickson joined the Episcopal congregation and in June 1763 entered into an agreement with them to extend his wall along the west side of their ground and to extend his bank and terrace across their property to the bridge, with full power to make a gate through for his pleasure or convenience. The new, but ill-fated, six-arch stone Kelso Bridge had been erected between 1756 and 1758 and access was situated behind St. Andrew's chapel, so by creating a short-cut to it James Dickson was well-placed when setting out on coach journeys to London and seems to have travelled the road quite frequently. The public coach at that time took three days and two nights to reach London from Edinburgh, with 27 stopping places en route through Morpeth, Newcastle, Durham, Doncaster, Grantham and Stevenage.

Old Kelso Bridge

James Dickson employed as his architect James Nisbet, a native of Kelso, whose practice was based in Berners Street, London, and he is suspected of borrowing ideas from Isaac Ware's "Complete Body of Architecture". Nisbet was also mentioned in George Ridpath's diary:

> *"March 1761 – [Sir Francis Blake of Twizel, related to the Collingwood family]...has at last fallen to work on the old*

house, which is to be repaired...for this purpose he has actually made a contract with Nisbet the mason, who is employed in building the new house at Paxton".

Nisbet was principal mason building the house of "Billy" near Coldingham, and went on to superintend the building of Wedderburn Castle to designs by Robert Adam. He built the octagonal Parish Church in Kelso in 1771 with the help of John Laidlaw, mason, and John Purves, carpenter. Nisbet died in 1781.

The best description of the exterior of Ednam House is to be found in "Kelso Records" by Mason, written in 1789:

> *"...a beautiful mansion, with pleasure ground, situated on a most healthful and pleasant bank, close by the side of the river, adorned with all that can please the eye or charm the senses; art and nature have both been explored to beautify this lovely spot...in the middle of the bank and pleasure ground which is smooth and even as a bowling green, stands the beautiful edifice, fitted up in highest taste, and furnished with every pleasurable ornament. All along, on each side, adjacent to the building, are elegant garden walls, ornamented in the finest manner with an arrangement of stone pillars. On top of these splendid walls are fine emblematical figures some representing men, some women, here and there disposed so as to make the habitation the more agreeable and to dazzle the beholder. On the cornice of the building are likewise curious figures, in perfect symmetry. In the midst of this delightful spot of ground, and elevated on two pedestals, are two beautiful statues, the one representing Jupiter and the other Diana; but particular notice is taken of a curious figure, a statue of a little black boy, in humble posture, kneeling upon one knee and holding a sundial with both hands upon the crown of his head. On the front of the bank are two spacious gravel walks, as straight as a line, about 230 paces long.*
>
> *...at the upper end of the same walk stands a green-house, supported with a range of fine stone pillars, with many costly ornaments, and furnished with a great variety of foreign plants and flowers; adjoining to which stands a hot-house, filled with clusters of richest vine. The whole is a finished picture of prosperity and grandeur and if well delineated, it would exhibit a picture which you might call romance, or the result of a*

visionary fancy. At the upper end of the other gravel walk stands a summer house likewise supported by a range of stone pillars; upon the top of the building stands a spruce statue. ....all round the bank are, here and there, beds of beautiful and variegated flowers, embroidered with greatest splendour...auriculas, carnations, tulips, violets, pinks, jessamine and woodbine".

Summer House at Ednam House Hotel after alteration

At the time that his mansion was built, James Dickson named it Havannah House, which indicates either that he had made a good deal of money from the enterprise, or that he had such pride in the outcome that he wished to commemorate it. Whatever the reason, it betrays a personal involement in the matter, perhaps because his nephew William was serving at that time under Sir George Pocock, who led the expedition, or perhaps because his friend Sir James Douglas had taken an active part. It wasn't until Dickson bought Ednam estate some years later that the name was changed to Ednam House, only Havannah Court now recalling the former name.

A more recent description of the house can be found in the Royal Commission records of the County of Roxburgh, which includes the following observations:

"The basement contains the kitchen and offices. The entrance opens into a square hall which has an enriched ceiling. On the North wall is a marble mantlepiece with a head

carved on the centre of the frieze – above is a trophy with enriched framework. Doorways on the North open on to the main stair; South to passage and service stair; West to dining-room. The finely modelled ceiling portrays Aurora in chariot and motifs taken from Aesops Fables. North – carved mantlepiece of marble and caryatids at the sides. Mahogany doors, elaboratlely carved, surmounted by broken pediments. A room at the North West corner of the house has modelled plaster ceiling representing Music, Sculpture, Painting. [Plasterwork by Thomas Perritt and Joseph Rose]. The coved frieze bears delicate enrichment with a moulded mantlepiece of red and white marble. South West corner - fine ceiling of modelled plaster. Mantlepiece of green, yellow and white marble. Plaster relief of Europa and the bull. The fretted brass door-furniture is noteworthy. The South-East corner – original plaster ceiling, enriched frieze. The main stair North East has turned mahogany balusters. The first floor has a pillared upper hall – square coving surmounted by lantern light".

At the time this description was written (1956) it was noted that the window above the entrance had been scratched by a diamond on the pane:

"Sept. 20th 1787 B. Dickson L. Sleath".

This was Betty or Elizabeth Dickson, second wife of William, celebrating her marriage of the previous day. "L. Sleath" may have been Betty's friend or bridesmaid, for William's will in 1801 names Rev. William Sleith of Ripton Priory in the County of Derby as a guardian to his children in the event of his death. Unfortunately, this very window-pane was accidentally broken some years ago. Below the window, in the pediment above the front door, is displayed the arms of James Dickson (not those of his wife) and the motto "Fortes Fortuna Juvat".

Ednam House must have been very conspicuous in eighteenth century Kelso, having such an imposing facade and magnificent grounds in comparison with the thatched houses, unpaved streets and generally unkempt appearance of the rest of the town. Mason notes that the gate of Ednam House in 1789 was next to Palmer's office in Bridge Street, (where it is today) but Wood's map of 1823 shows the gateway at the South East corner of the grounds, entering Abbey Court, with a high wall along the Bridge Street side.

James Dickson entertained quite lavishly, including among his guests John, the young bachelor Duke of Roxburghe. The family at Floors Castle had not had a happy relationship with the town of Kelso for some time, and it is reputed that Duke John avoided the townspeople whenever possible, drawing the blinds of his coach and driving fast over Kelso Bridge. James Dickson had a scheme for projecting a canal between Berwick and Kelso and started a subscription list to promote it. He first handed the paper to the Duke, who promised £200, but this comparatively small sum from the most prestigious patron would not have encouraged the lesser contributors and Dickson, realising his cause was lost, cast the list into the fire. His foresight was recognised later, when in 1790 the idea of a canal was reviewed and Mr. Whitworth was asked to survey land between Berwick and Ancrum Bridge, up the Tweed and crossing to Teviot. A committee was appointed for conducting the canal, abridging the former plan, and Mr. Whitworth reported back. The plan was approved, the committee was to circulate papers and raise funds, but the project seems to have suffered the same fate as James Dickson's proposal.

The kitchen garden of Ednam House was situated some distance away, where Grove House now stands on Edenside Road, opposite Tait Hall. The land formed that part of the Tofts which had belonged to John Jamieson, who owned an extensive farm in the 17th Century. It was enclosed by a ditch and hedge with a wall on the south side and a "house and shades built thereon". According to legend, James Dickson allowed his favourite slave to grow tobacco there. Certainly tobacco was grown in Kelso at that time, notably by Dr. Charles Jackson of Nicolatownfield (later Rosebank), and a drying-house for leaves gave its name to Drying House Lane.

When James Dickson died in 1771, his nephew William inherited Ednam House and its kitchen garden, but his widow Betty inherited the liferent of the whole furniture...plate...jewels "within my house at Kelso" and £400 per year for life. Mrs. Dickson stayed on at Ednam House for some time and continued to worship in St. Andrew's Church. In June 1778, the chapel minutes show that the committee was anxious to remove a dunghill which was now "lying about the entry, occasioned chiefly by weeds and stuff from Mrs. Dickson's garden". The committee agreed to pay a labourer for its removal and to ask Mrs. Dickson to give orders to prevent a recurrence. At this time also, the minutes record that Ednam House was being advertised for sale in the papers and there was concern about the arrangement with the late Mr. Dickson which had allowed him to encroach on the chapel grounds. Captain William Dickson was contacted and appeared at the next meeting with the paper containing the original contract. After hearing that James Dickson had contributed £20 towards the erection of the chapel and the building of a dyke to hold back the Tweed, besides making an annual donation towards its upkeep, those present unanimously approved the continuation of the agreement. Mrs. Dickson's name no longer appears after 1787, when her newly-wed namesake, Betty Dickson, engraved her name in the window.

William Dickson sold the estate at Ednam that year to Arthur Cuthbert from Woodcotpark, Surrey, whose son, James Ramsay Cuthbert inherited when Arthur died in 1792. James R. Cuthbert then purchased Ednam House from William Dickson, with James Watt, merchant in Kelso, acting as his procurator and attorney. Mr. Cuthbert wrote in May 1792 to the treasurer of St. Andrew's, James Palmer, asking for the opinion of the chapel managers with regard to raising the dyke between the chapel and the river and putting a new rail on top, but by November he had changed his mind. However, it did prompt the managers to ask for an acknowledgement of their agreement with James Dickson and to attempt to regain their property to avoid any inconvenience.

In 1799, Mr. Cuthbert sold on the mansion house, gardens, kitchen garden with gardener's and coachman's houses to Mr. Andrew Douglas of Portland Place and of Burton in the County of Buckinghamshire. The deeds mention a piece of ground south of the tenement adjacent which once belonged to Charles Ormiston, then Andrew Watson, surgeon and "now consists of a paved area on the outside of the wall and a large gate leading to the said mansion (Ednam) house; it shall not be in the power of Andrew Douglas or his successors to shut up any windows in the gavel of the said tenement fronting the piece of ground". Permission was retained to place ladders for mending the roof.

Andrew Douglas was the son of George Douglas, who had been born in Fort William in 1711, and his wife Margaret Collis. Their elder son Christopher became a doctor, in 1769 married Pringle Home, daughter of George Home of Bassendean, and settled in Kelso. Andrew Douglas appears to have been a wealthy man for, in 1803, he subscribed £21.0.0 towards the Volunteer Force when other men, including his brother, were donating £10.0.0. He died in 1806, a year after Dr. Christopher, and his widow, Mary Sharp, became owner of Ednam House. After Andrew's death, Henry Swan, writer, arranged for his widow the acquisition of another piece of waste ground, probably behind the weigh-house, as it had been purchased in 1738 by the Duke of Roxburghe from Alexander Scott of Thirlestane and Walter Scott of Harden. Mary only survived her husband by eight months, but she appears to have been well-regarded according to her headstone in the grounds of St. Andrew's church. It was erected in her memory by "William Hammond, Esq., of St. Alban's Court, who profited by her example". Walter Riddell Carre, in his book "Border Memories", states that Mrs. Douglas of Ednam House published "The Life of Gellert", about an eminent German poet and writer, with a course of moral lessons taken from a French translation of the original German.

The new Kelso Bridge by Rennie had just been built, the previous one having been swept away during floods in 1797. An early example of compulsory purchase was made when the Convener and Deacons of Trades in Kelso were involved in a decision to widen the road leading to the bridge. This included demolition of a previously ruined half-tenement and yard which had belonged to James Dickson, and property which belonged to two sisters, Elizabeth Fraser and Helen Home. They were daughters of Andrew Robertson, who had returned to set up as a merchant in Kelso after a sojourn in Calcutta and the East Indies. Their brother Andrew, of the 58th Regiment of Foot, had died, as had Elizabeth's husband William Fraser, a captain in the 42nd Regiment. Helen was married to James Home, writer, and lived at Roxburgh House.

Mary Douglas left instructions that Ednam House should pass to her nephew, Dr. James Douglas, son of Dr. Christopher. James had spent some time in Reading, Berkshire, before returning to his inheritance at Kelso, which included a house in the Market Place, left to him by his father. He and his wife, Frances Robson of Samieston, moved into Ednam House and their son Francis was born there in 1815. However, James and Frances decided to build a new house for themselves east of the churchyard, later known as Abbey Bank, and in August 1818 Ednam House and its policies were put up for sale. While waiting to move into their new house, the Douglas family occupied part of the Cross Keys Hotel property in Market Place.

The man who now purchased Ednam House was Mr. John Robertson, a merchant in Threadneedle Street, London, but originally from Kelso. His sister Margaret was married to Samuel Robertson, the brewer at Ednam, and there was close contact between the two families. In 1808, John Roberston married Margaretta Jane Miller, whose father, William Miller, was a Commander in the Royal Navy. Her mother was Margaret Dickson, eldest daughter of the Rev. George Dickson of Bedrule and her uncle, David Dickson, was a naval surgeon and Inspector of Fleets and Hospitals, later given a knighthood. Margaret Miller had a small fortune of her own and she and the children existed on this while her husband was at sea, living firstly at Maxwellheugh and then in Belmount Place. Margaretta was born in Berwick in 1786 and the Old Parish Records for Kelso show that she had a brother, George, born in 1789 and a sister, Wilhelmina, in 1791. When Margaret died aged 40, in 1805, she was buried in Kelso churchyard and Margaretta took charge of the family. William Miller was promoted and took a house at Portsmouth; the family moved there and he remarried. After Margaretta married John Robertson, who was 20 years her senior, they travelled extensively before purchasing Ednam House and settling in Kelso.

John Robertson also bought an old enclosed flower-garden known as Dr. Ormston's, next to Bridge Street and south of a house still owned by Dr. Douglas. To this he added the weigh-house and machine, which he purchased from the Duke of Roxburghe, and part of this was fitted up as a dwelling-house and rented out at a total of £42 per annum. He demolished part of the wall separating the two areas to make a stance for carts and waggons fronting Bridge Street. Dr. Douglas had added to the Ednam House policies by purchasing from the trustees the piece of ground which had formed the eastern approach to the old bridge, so the total area was now quite extensive. Besides, there was still the kitchen garden at the east end of the town and this was tenanted by a William Matthew.

It was around this time that Margaretta's sister married William Shedden of Wimpole Street, a partner in the firm of Messrs Hawthorn and Shedden, West India Merchants of Lime St. Square, London. William had originally been in the navy during the Napoleonic wars and his son Robert also went to sea, was involved in the Chinese wars, and in 1841 was master of the "James Lyon", a brigantine in the Liverpool-Honduras trade. John Robertson was fond of his wife's nephew Robert Shedden and bequeathed to him his gold repeating watch as a mark of his affection.

When Mr Robertson died on 27th February 1842, his obituary indicated a deep religious faith:

> *"After languishing many months he sunk to rest in perfect resignation to the will of God and in the fullest hope of future and eternal happiness through the merits of a Redeemer. He longed to be united to his Saviour and his God".*

He was attended during his last illness by Dr. James Douglas, physician, and John Stuart, surgeon in Kelso.

His widow requested permission of the committee of St. Andrew's Church to erect a mural monument, but a marble tombstone was not permitted as it might cause an obstruction. The tablet must have been transferred when the chapel was later rebuilt.

Ednam House Hotel, pre-1928

John Robertson was an extremely wealthy man and amongst his bequests was the sum of £200 to be distributed by the Kirk Session to the poor of Kelso. It was thought that he had invested £1,000 in shares for the building of Waterloo Bridge in London, which of course was modelled on Kelso Bridge. However, he had considered this "a very bad concern and most of it would be thrown away", and no record of such an investment was found. Beneficiaries of his will included his sister Janet Stewart and her daughter Helen, who had married General Malkowski of Budweiss, Bohemia. There were details of bonds which he had granted to the Earl of Seafield and his son, Lord Reidhaven; to John Waldie the banker and John Waldie of Hendersyde; and to his nephew, Peter Robertson, who had disponed property including a dwelling-house and brewery on the north side of Oven Wynd. One small task which fell to John Robertson's widow was the cancellation of his standing order for the "London Evening Chronicle" which he had with Halliburton, the bookseller in Coldstream.

In 1847, Mrs. Robertson's nephew Robert Shedden bought his own schooner, the "Nancy Dawson", which was built in Gosport, carried on a coasting and foreign trade, and was the first schooner of its size (164 tons) to circum-navigate the globe. A year later, the "Nancy Dawson" was heading for Siberia via the Loo Choo Islands, well-stocked with provisions and crewed to over-capacity, mainly with Americans. At this time several ships were searching for Sir John Franklin, who had disappeared without trace while leading an expedition to find the North West passage around America in the ships "Terror" and "Erebus". Some evidence was found quite recently to suggest their probable fate. When Captain Henry Kellett in H.M.S. Herald arrived in July 1849 at Awachta Bay near Petropavlovska, he was greatly surprised to find the "Nancy Dawson" flying the burgee of the Royal Thames Yacht Club, its commander volunteering his services to assist in the search despite the fact that he was in the last stages of consumption. Robert Shedden asked Kellett if he could have a naval officer on board, but he was in independent command of his vessel when "Nancy Dawson" accompanied the "Herald" out of the Bay, parting from her a month later. He met up with the "Plover" and her Commander Moore and followed the "Plover"'s boats up to Point Barrow, ran aground on a shoal but managed to get off again. It was then that the crew began to mutiny and told Shedden that they would "do for him" if they were forced to winter there. The second master of the "Plover" was called over and had three men put in irons, but there were other refusals to obey orders. Shedden decided to sail southward and eventually sighted the "Herald" and Captain Kellett took the three men off, ordering his second master to take charge of the "Nancy Dawson" and sail to Mazatlan to await the arrival of the "Herald".

Robert Shedden died there, aged 29. In 1851, a tablet was erected to his memory in the Church of Weston Underwood in Buckinghamshire, extolling his bravery.

Meanwhile, in Kelso, his aunt Robertson was also honouring his memory. A piece of land at the eastern end of Horsemarket in Kelso, forming part of the "Short Whaings", was advertised for sale in the paper and Mrs. Robertson sent home to have it purchased. During the following year she bought two other fields and gave £500 to be "expended on embellishment and beautifying". The rough surface was transformed, with the assistance of local farmers who lent men and ploughs. The result was a fine Public Park, known as Shedden Park, gifted to the people of Kelso. A handsome gateway and railings were erected by public subscription and Mr. Tait, nurseryman, gifted trees and shrubs. A lodge was built for the keeper of the park, who received £10 per annum in addition to the free house. In 1860, the flagpole from the "Nancy Dawson" was erected alongside the Lodge and remained there until the 1950s. Mrs. Robertson later gifted a number of dwelling-houses and gardens in Rose Lane, the rents of which would finance the maintenance of the park. Trustees were appointed to administer the funds, and in 1863 they decided they had enough money to build a band-stand.

The official opening of Shedden Park took place in November 1851 amid public rejoicing on a large scale. The Commissioners of Police, the Convenory of the Incorporated Trades and the Merchant Company of Kelso all made presentations to Mrs. Robertson at Ednam House, partaking of cake and wine after her reply. The inauguration dinner at the Cross Keys Hotel was sold out and a second one was accommodated at the Queens Head. The Tweed-side Cricket Club and friends held their own dinner at the White Swan, while the Quoiting Club met at the Salmon Inn in Mill Wynd. Mrs. Robertson's coachman, George Anderson, and a cabinet-maker called John McDougall were entertained to supper in the Weigh House in Bridge Street in recognition of their efforts in decorating the town, particularly for the triumphal arch over Havannah Close. By public subscription, a portrait of Mrs. Robertson was painted, to be hung in the Town Hall. A further proof of Mrs. Robertson's popularity was provided the following August. She returned to Kelso accompanied by her sister-in-law, Mrs. Frederick Miller, having been abroad over the winter for the good of her health, and was cheered through the streets by the townsfolk. Shedden Park was, and still is, of enormous benefit to Kelsonians, who use it for a variety of recreational pursuits, from sports to concerts. In 1855, it was used as a parade ground by the militia who were in training for the Crimean war. The men were billeted on private families in Kelso or stayed in the fever wards of the Dispensary until the Malt Barns in Mayfield were converted into temporary barracks. The cannons from the "Nancy Dawson" were lent by Mrs. Robertson to mark the visit of the Prince and Princess of Wales in 1865 and that of Queen Victoria in 1867. They were a fixed feature of Shedden Park within living memory, but mysteriously disappeared along with the flagpole. The Trustees of Shedden Park handed over responsibility to the Town Council on it's centenary in 1950.

Although Mrs. Robertson spent a good deal of time abroad in Europe, mainly for health reasons, she was always generous to poor people in Kelso and sent money to Mr. Aitchison, Inspector of the Poor, to be distributed. Her sister, Mrs. Shedden, also donated £40 for the destitute in 1836, part to be used to purchase meal. This generosity was continual, for in 1870 Mrs. Robertson was giving her annual gift of £50 to be distributed by Mr. Moscrip, the Supt. of Police. She entertained the children from the Ragged School on special occasions and left them an annuity after her death.

Mrs. Robertson gave employment to many people, including Margaret Jerdan who was with her for 27 years, dying in 1853 after a long and painful illness. Her butler, George Cassy, was originally from Duns and he lived with his wife and family at Ednam House until his death in 1862. His successor, William Buchell, also died three years later, aged only 25. Both of them are buried in Kelso Abbey churchyard. Young artists found in Mrs. Robertson a generous patron and she adorned the walls of Ednam House with their works; in 1851 she gifted a painting to the Scottish National Gallery. When St. Andrew's Episcopal Church alongside was replaced by a larger building in 1868, Mrs. Robertson not only allowed encroachment on the grounds of Ednam House but also donated a new organ, a brass eagle lectern and a stained-glass window to the church.

At the time the 1871 Census was taken, Mrs. Robertson, then aged 84, had her half-sister, Madeleine Miller, aged 41, staying with her at Ednam House. Four years later, Madeleine married Henri de Tourville who passed himself off as a Count in order to attract a rich wife. The following year, he pushed poor Madeleine over a precipice at Stelvio Pass in the Tyrol. At his trial, it transpired that he had poisoned his first wife by putting powdered glass in her food and drink; he was accused of shooting his mother-in-law; and he had set fire to his house to kill his only child, by whose death he stood to gain a large sum of money. He was imprisoned for life and died in 1890.

For the last five years of her life, blindness curtailed Mrs. Robertson's activities and she didn't venture outside the gates of Ednam House, but remained cheerful. On 29th November 1872, she was found dead in bed. Exactly a year later, a deed of directions was drawn up to dispose of her considerable property.

The Duke of Roxburghe's mother was at that time occupying the Dower House at Dunbar, but the Duke himself did not enjoy good health and thought a second Dower House might be required for his own use. With this in mind, he purchased Ednam House from the Trustees of Mrs. Robertson, but died at Genoa in 1879 without ever taking occupation. His son, the 7th Duke, leased Ednam House and the 1881 census lists the occupants as Mr. John Drummond from Edinburgh, his wife Emma and mother-in-law Mrs. Augusta Thornton. Mr. Drummond gave his age as 38, but ten years later it had jumped to 50; even so, the Census recorder noted in pencil "ages appear to be much under-stated". Another discrepancy occured in Mrs. Emma Drummond's place of birth, which in 1881 was given as England, but had changed by 1891 to Paris. No doubt there was a simple explanation for both facts! The 7th Duke died at the early age of 53 in 1892, but Ednam House continued to be occupied by Mrs. Drummond as a widow until 1927, when she too died and the property was advertised for sale.

Ednam House was converted into an unlicensed hotel in 1928 under the ownership of Mr. Ralph Brooks, with his son Ralph as manager. They made considerable improvements to provide modern facilities, such as the installation of electric light and added bathrooms. In 1931, a guest could rent a room for 5s. 6d. a night (27p!) and have breakfast for 3/-. Garage accommodation, including lock-ups, were available at a cost of 2/- per night for the duration of the visit and a skilled mechanic was in attendance to do running repairs. The hotel has always been particularly attractive to fishermen, but it is a very popular venue for the community of Kelso and hosts a variety of events, great and small.

Over the intervening years necessary extensions have been built, but the character of the house has fortunately been retained with the original doorways and wonderful plaster ceilings still intact. Alastair Brooks, grandson of the original proprietor, his wife Sheila and their son, Ralph, are the current custodians of the treasure that is Ednam House. The arms of James Dickson are still visible above the main door and he gazes down benevolently from his portrait in the hall on all who enter.

CHAPTER THREE - SOURCES

Kelso Records – Mason

Borders & Berwick – Charles Strang

Old Parish Records

Records of St. Andrew's Church

Census Records

Register of Sasines

Maritime Museum, Greenwich

Ridpath's Diary

Royal Commission of Ancient Monuments in Scotland

History of Roxburghshire – Jeffrey

Somerville's Life and Times

Kelso Mail

Ledger of Ednam House Trust

Brochure of Ednam House Hotel, 1931

FAMILY TREE SHOWING DICKSON - MURRAY LINK

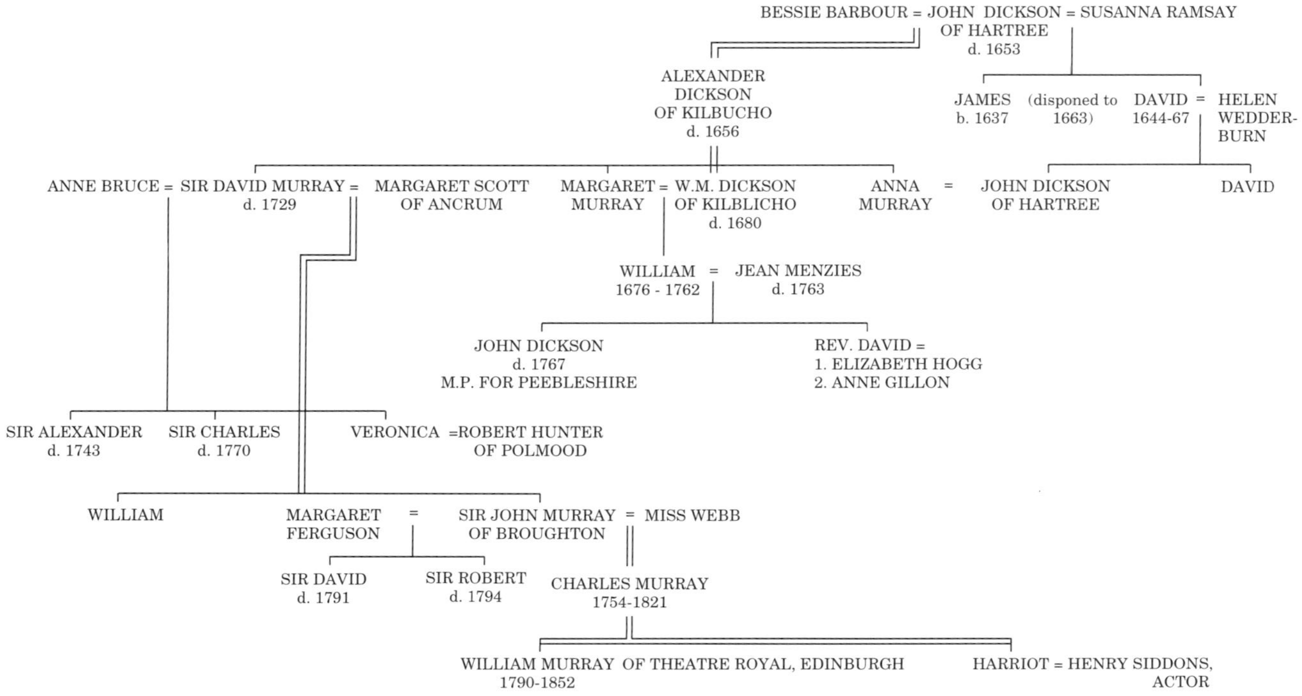

CHAPTER FOUR

BROUGHTON

When James Dickson was three years old, a son, John, was born to Sir David Murray of Stanhope and his second wife, Margaret Scott of Ancrum, whose life was to affect thousands of his countrymen. John Murray was educated at the universities of Edinburgh and Leyden before spending some time in Rome. James Murray, brother to Sir David, had been gentleman of the bedchamber to James VII, and John Murray his nephew became close to the House of Stuart, living in exile in Rome but planning to return with a vengeance in the near future. When he returned to Scotland in 1738, John Murray made the acquaintance of other prominent Jacobite supporters and acted as a liaison between them in several countries. He married Margaret Ferguson, daughter of Col. Robert Ferguson of Nithsdale, and it is reported that this fiery lady sat on horseback at the Mercat Cross of Edinburgh, cockade in hat and sword in hand, welcoming recruits to the Jacobite cause.

The Barony of Broughton, ten miles up the river Tweed from Peebles, had belonged to the Murrays until 1719, when Alexander Murray, older half-brother to John, sold it to John Douglas, brother of the Earl of March, who had an arrangement of mutual entail with another brother, James Douglas of Stow. Both John and James Douglas died before 1734 and their nephew, the second Earl of March, a minor at the time, inherited the debt-laden estate. For the benefit of creditors the property was exposed for sale and there was only one offer – from William Veitch, W.S., acting on behalf of John Murray, eldest surviving son of Sir David Murray by his second marriage – and thenceforth John was known as Murray of Broughton.

Murray joined Prince Charles Edward Stuart in France in 1744 and was with him at Holyrood Palace in Edinburgh in the autumn of 1745, when he prevailed upon the directors of the Royal Bank of Scotland to convert banknotes into coin for payment of the Highland Army. Four days after the tragedy of Culloden, Prince Charlie left Moidart in an open boat but John Murray was not fit enough to travel with him. Instead, he joined Cameron of Lochiel and Major Kennedy in flight on the hillsides, starving, wandering by night between scouts and never sleeping anywhere for two nights in succession. Murray promised to pay arrears to the clans who had been defeated in the '45 and is said to have buried 3 parcels of Louis d'Ors in a wood beside Loch Arkaig for safe-keeping. Attempting to rejoin the Prince in Uist, Murray again fell ill, but planned to sail for Holland with Lochiel. To make his way to Leith, he disguised himself as a drover and travelled through Glen Lyon, Balquhidder and Carnwath to Kilbucho in Peeblesshire, where he had relatives.

Kilbucho House

William Dickson of Kilbucho was the son of William Dickson and his wife Margaret, sister to Sir David Murray of Stanhope, and therefore cousin to John Murray. It was Friday, 27th June 1746 when John Murray arrived at Kilbucho Place; his appearance aroused the suspicions of a servant, who reported him to the dragoons. Meanwhile Murray moved on to nearby Polmood, the home of his half-sister Veronica, Mrs. Hunter, where he fell into an exhausted sleep. There he was captured by dragoons under Sergeant John Smith, whose company, ironically, was based at Murray's own house at Broughton. He was taken first to Edinburgh, imprisoned in the Castle, and thence by coach to the Tower of London. During his trial before the Duke of Newcastle, Murray of Broughton turned

King's Evidence and betrayed his former friends and conspirators. He was released in 1748 with a pension of £200 and a reputation which earned him contempt amounting to hate by friend and foe alike. Two years later, in the final and complex transactions involving heritable bonds, the Earl of March served himself heir to John Douglas under a mutual entail of 1725 and granted a conveyance to John Murray: the purchase of Broughton was completed. In August 1750, Murray paid a heritable bond of £3,000 sterling to John Ferguson, Esq., Commander of H.M. Ship of War, the "Porcupine", with "£600 liquidate expenses in case of taillie".

John Murray did carry out improvements on his estate at Broughton, particularly on the farms of Upper and Nether Mains. Here he divided the arable land with dykes and ditches; he also altered the course of Broughton burn to prevent flooding of the meadows. Along with William Dickson of Kilbucho he made a new course for Biggar Water, between the Skirling and Dreva marches.

The estate of Broughton came up for sale in 1764, at a time when James Dickson was looking for investments for his considerable fortune. He instructed his notary, Walter Scott, at that time living in College Wynd in Edinburgh, to arrange the purchase with Thomas Tod, W.S. who was acting for John Murray. In his biography "Life of Sir Walter Scott", J.G. Lockhart describes a famous incident which occured at this time:

> *"Mrs. Scott's curiosity was strongly excited one autumn by the regular appearance, at a certain hour every evening, of a sedan chair, to deposit a person carefully muffled up in a mantle, who was immediately ushered into her husband's private room, and commonly remained with him there until long after the usual bed-time of this orderly family. Mr. Scott answered her repeated inquiries with a vagueness which irritated the lady's feelings more and more: until, at last, she could bear the thing no longer; but one evening, just as she heard the bell ring as for the stranger's chair to carry him off, she made her appearance within the forbidden parlour with a salver in her hand, observing, that she thought the gentlemen had sat so long, they would be the better of a dish of tea, and had ventured accordingly to bring some for their acceptance. The stranger,a person of distinguished appearance, and richly dressed, bowed to the lady, and accepted a cup; but her husband knit his brows, and refused very coldly to partake*

the refreshment. A moment afterwards the visitor withdrew – and Mr. Scott lifting up the window-sash, took the cup, which he had left empty on the table, and tossed it out upon the pavement. The lady exclaimed for her china, but was put to silence by her husband's saying, "I can forgive your little curiosity, madam, but you must pay the penalty. I may admit to my house, on a piece of business, persons wholly unworthy to be treated as guests by my wife. Neither lip of me nor of mine comes after Mr. Murray of Broughton's".

James Dickson had spent so much time in London that he may not have shared the depth of antipathy towards John Murray which was felt by his solicitor. Anna Murray, a sister of Sir David Murray of Stanhope, had married John Dickson of Hartree, so John Murray had relations who might also have been connected to James Dickson. (see family tree) If Dickson really was connected to the Dicksons of Kilbucho, he may have heard through them that the estate was available for purchase. John Dickson of Kilbucho was witness to an arrangement between James Dickson and his nephew William in September 1764. Another possibility lies in contact through the Freemasons, as John Murray had joined in 1737 and was affiliated to Lodge Canongate Kilwinning no. 2 in Edinburgh, while James Dickson was Senior Grand Warden of the Grand Lodge of English Freemasons before being elected Grand Master in Kelso. In later years, the name of Murray was obliterated wherever it appeared in the Lodge's transactions.

On 17th May 1764, in London, John Rutherford, apprentice to Walter Scott, recorded the sale as follows:

"Disponed by John Murray to James Dickson – delivered up by order of James Dickson to Walter Scott, writer to the signet, agent for his behoof...and in the custody of Charles Murray of Stanhope [half-brother to John] as being part of progress of writs of the said estate.

Witness Albert Innes, merchant
John Davies, clerk to James Dickson"

Contrasting styles of signature on the Broughton document.

The price was £16,000 sterling, but of that £4,075 was to be paid within six months after the death of John Murray's wife, Margaret Ferguson. Mrs. Murray had been pregnant at the time of Culloden and she too fled after the battle, being given shelter at a succession of safe houses including the home of her mother in Cant's Close, Edinburgh. She gave birth to a son, Charles, in September 1746, but he died as an infant. Having made several unsuccessful attempts to sail to Holland from Leith, Margaret Murray travelled to London where she lived in Newport Street, Lambeth, under an assumed name. Eventually she did reach the Continent, but little is known of her fate. John Murray's eldest son David succeeded his father in 1777 as Laird of Stanhope. In 1786, when he was living at Kirkby Street, Hatton Garden, London, David appointed Archibald Mercer of Edinburgh as factor to receive the £4,075 bond from James Dickson's heir, his mother being deceased.

Avenue of trees leading to Broughton Place

No picture now exists of the house at Broughton, which was formerly known as "Littlehope", but it was described as "a good mansion house" and stood almost in the same spot as the existing Broughton Place, with the same avenue of trees approaching it. At the beginning of September, 1764, James Dickson granted to his nephew, William Dickson, R.N., the lands of Over and Nether

Stirkfields, Clashieford, houses, biggings, yards, mosses, muirs, marches, common pasturage, and meadows lying within the Barony of Broughton, and part of the dominant lands of Broughtonshiels, all contained in the bond due to Margaret Murray. However, within days, William was disponing the same lands, with the pertinents, for "certain onerous causes" in favour of James Dickson once more. This was witnessed by John Dickson of Kilbucho, Richard Gillespie, tacksman, and Walter Scott. James Dickson added to his possessions the following year by purchasing the other part of Broughton Shiels from John Porteous, "with the right to ten soums (units of pasturage) on the common, the pasturage of a mare and foal, and a brood sow, and the right of digging and winning peats and turf." John Porteous remained as tenant in part of Broughton Shiels, with Alexander Carrick in the other part. There were other tenants in the town of Broughton; in Cloverhill; in the Mill of Broughton; in half of Burnetland; in Langlaw-hill, Know and Deandyke; in Stirkfield and the Upper and Nether Mains; and in Rottenraw. There were houses, one with a shop, another with a smithy – all paying rent in proportion to their value, giving Dickson a good income. In 1767, he took proceedings to have the teinds valued, and obtained a decree of valuation against the Hon. Mrs. Clementina Fleming, wife of the Hon. Charles Elphinstone, and against Rev. Andrew Plummer, the minister, for his interest. The following year, he raised an action to determine the proper division of the lands of Burnetland, one half of which belonged to him, and the other half to Patrick Sibbald, wright in Edinburgh, and his sister Jean, wife of James Lorimer, the minister at Yarrow. The Sheriff-Depute, Andrew Murray of Cringletie, decreed that 63.22 acres on the East belonged to the Sibbalds, and the 121.69 acres remaining belonged to James Dickson.

On a lighter note, there were old ruins, the remains of ten castles, among which were reputed to be the foundations of "Macbeth's Castle", on Dickson's land. They were described thus: "In the under story they had a wooden door of uncommon thickness, full of iron spikes with broad heads, and a strong iron gate that opened in the inside: one of these doors and gates was preserved in the parish for a long time as a piece of antiquity". Dickson employed workmen to dig in search of treasure or antiquities but they found only some coins and pieces of armour.

In 1765, James Dickson purchased from the Bank of Scotland an Heritable Bond for £3,500 with interest twice a year, which

William Dickson of Kilbucho and his son John had borrowed in June 1746, after Culloden. Although there is no evidence that William Dickson was an active Jacobite, he tried unsuccessfully to claim £1,000 as compensation for loss of regality priveleges on the abolition of heritable jurisdictions in 1747. By 1765 William Dickson had died and his eldest son John, an advocate, had succeeded. He had been the member of Parliament for Peeblesshire since 1747 and was "among the Scots friends of the Administration", but not specifically attached to the Duke of Argyll. He supported the plan for a Scots Militia and was nominated by a committee to prepare a bill, which was aborted in 1760. John Dickson was eager to leave Parliament if someone would be kind enough to bestow an office on him. He was made an offer which he refused in the hope that his chances would be improved after the imminent election. Originally supportive of the Bute administration, he transferred his allegiance to Grenville when, as Laird of Kilbucho, he aspired to higher pretensions. He lost out on a small post in the Mint which James Stuart Mackenzie might have created for him. He died un-married in 1767 and his heir was his brother, Rev. David Dickson, despite John's efforts to prevent him from succeeding. Initially trained for the law, David Dickson switched to the church and became minister of Newlands in 1755. Described as a "quarrelsome fellow", his career as a minister was a stormy one and he abandoned the church living when he became, in his turn, Laird of Kilbucho, and had the patronage of the church in that parish. David Dickson also tried to serve himself heir to his father when his relations at Whitslade fell into debt to Kilbucho in 1770, but he was thwarted in this attempt by his cousin selling to another relation in Somerset. In that year, James Dickson sold the Heritable Bond which he held over Kilbucho, and one wonders whether he gave David Dickson the option of redeeming it first. It passed to James Ker, the eldest son of Alexander Ker, who had been a merchant in Bordeaux and Montpellier in France. In the absence of his father, James Ker was "pupil" to Sir William Forbes, Bart., James Hunter and John Stephen, merchants in Edinburgh, and Walter Scott, W.S., who of course was Dickson's solicitor. The transaction took place in London, witnessed by Captain William Dickson, Neil McVicar, merchant in Edinburgh and Albert Innes, merchant in London. In 1768, James Dickson himself became Member of Parliament for the four-town district of Linlithgow, Selkirk, Lanark, and Peebles, known as Linlithgow Burghs. His parliamentary career, however, was undistinguished and cut short by his death.

At Broughton, considerable improvements were carried out in Dickson's time and he rebuilt the village "in the English fashion" – very neat. He was described as "a gentleman whose memory must ever be dear to the sons of Tweed, and although no living monument has yet been raised to perpetuate his munificence and public spirit, he will always be remembered as the patron of every polite and liberal art". Two hundred and more years later, there is still no monument and precious little memory!

As James and Betty Dickson had no children of their own, nephew and heir Captain William Dickson occupied Broughton Place for a time. His eldest son, William, was born in the house in 1770 and in November the following year he succeeded to the property on the death of his uncle James. Archibald Collingwood Dickson was also born at Broughton in 1772, but owing to the carelessness of a servant the house was burned down a year later and not rebuilt. The Dickson family moved to Sydenham, near Kelso, and once again Broughton came up for sale.

The property was described in the "Edinburgh Advertiser":

"The Lands and Barony of Broughton, in the Parish of Broughtoun and shire of Peebles, consisting of 3,567 Scots acres, or thereby, mostly arable, and whereof about 400 acres are inclosed, and properly subdivided; all the inclosures being sufficiently fenced and supplied with water, and well sheltered by hedges and strips planted with thriving trees.

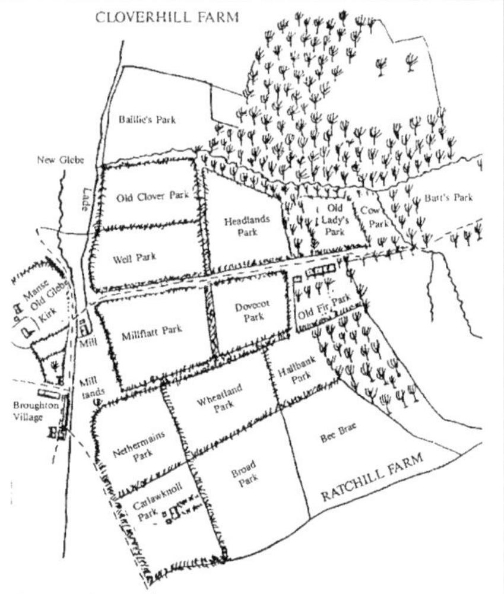

Broughton Estate 1799

This estate is capable of great improvement, and lies within a moderate distance of lime. The lands hold of the Crown and the yearly free rent is 716 l. Sterling, exclusive of kains and carriages not rentalled, and the valued rent, conform to which they pay rent and other public burdens, is 1083 l. 4s.8d Scots.

Broughtoun is 19 computed miles from Edinburgh, 8 from Peebles and 3 from Biggar; at which two last mentioned are exceeding good weekly markets for all kinds of grain.

There is upon the estate a neat village, newly erected and well inhabited with useful hands for carrying on all sorts of improvements.

There are sundry very large plantations of trees upon the estate, some of them being 30 years old and upwards, and well fenced and in a thriving condition and in the present lease the proprietor has reserved power to take off the farms in different places about 85 acres for planting, without making any allowance to the tenants. The tenants' houses are all newly fitted up and repaired and are mostly covered with blue slate and the church, manse and schoolhouse have likewise been of late thoroughly repaired.

William Bertram, merchant in Broughtoun, will show the premises. The progress of writs, which is clear, together with a plan of the estate with the rental thereof and tacks, may be seen in the hands of Walter Scott, Writer to the Signet, or the proprietor at Broughton-house, to either of whom persons intending to purchase may apply."

The estate was exposed to public voluntary roup in the Exchange Coffee-house in Edinburgh on 21st June and was registered in November 1774 to the new owner, Robert McQueen, Esquire, advocate, later Lord Braxfield, the inspiration for R.L. Stevenson's unfinished story "The Weir of Hermiston". Robert McQueen was then 52 years old and had been an advocate for 30. He made his mark by building a reputation as a sound lawyer and powerful pleader in handling the intricate and feudal questions which arose out of the forfeitures of the 1745 rebellion. In 1764, he succeeded Pitfour as chamber counsel and was elevated to the bench as Lord Braxfield in 1776. His home in Edinburgh until 1773 was in part of a mansion in Covenant Close, situated in High Street between Parliament Close and the Tron, but in that year he moved to no. 28 George Square, Walter Scott W.S. being his neighbour in no. 25. So close was his connection with the Scott family, that young Walter, on admission to the Faculty of Advocates in 1792, dedicated his Latin Thesis, "De Cadaveribus Damnatorum", to Lord Braxfield in flattering terms. Not everyone held him in high regard, however, for his manner was rough and he spoke in the Scots tongue. Lord Henry Cockburn was one of his detractors, describing him as

> *"Strong-built and dark with rough eyebrows, powerful eyes, threatening lips and a growling voice, he was like a formidable blacksmith....illiterate and without any taste for refined enjoyment, strength of understanding, which gave him power without cultivation, only encouraged him to a more contemptuous disdain of all natures less coarse than his own".*

If there were those who despised him for this, he was equally scathing about members of the Junior Bar who affected an Anglicised accent and he terrorised the "bar flunkies". Nevertheless, he was honest and kind-hearted, particularly towards young and nervous advocates making their first appearance. His sayings were legendary and he is credited with having addressed a man who made a very able speech in his own defence:

> *"There's nae doot ye're a vera clever chiel, man, but for a' that, I'm thinkin' ye wad be nane the waur o' a hanging".*

Broughton Place today

In March 1775, a Sasine was registered in favour of Francis Scott, brother of Walter Scott of Harden, giving the estate at Broughton as security against an heritable bond for £3,000, discharged in 1777. Lord Braxfield also bought adjacent land from John Porteous.

In the Statistical Account written in 1793 by Thomas Gray, the minister, the population of Broughton was given as 264, a drop of 103 since 1755. There were 20 dwelling-houses in the village, and 12 farmers in the parish; 4 weavers; 1 tailor; 1 smith; 1 miller; 2 shoemakers and 3 shop-keepers.

Braxfield held the office of Lord Justice-Clerk from 1788-99 although, due to illness, he was unable to attend court for the last year. He died in May 1799 and was buried in Lanark. He was succeeded by his son, Robert Dundas McQueen, who in 1803 also sought a decreet of valuation against Lord Elphinstone and others. The Broughton Place estate remained in the McQueen family until 1921, when the various properties were put up for sale. The farms were purchased by their tenants and the houses in the village were sold to individual buyers.

In 1936, Daniel Tudhope, solicitor in Edinburgh, disponed Broughton Place to Professor Thomas and Mrs. Sara Elliott, who commissioned Basil Spence, a young Edinburgh architect, to build a house in the style of the Scottish tower house of the 16th century. The result is so authentic that one might assume that this was the house occupied by James Dickson in 1764.

CHAPTER FOUR - SOURCES

History of Peeblesshire – Buchan.

History of Peeblesshire – Chambers

Annals of a Tweeddale Parish – Andrew Baird

Murray of Broughton's Memorials

A Living Village – Andrew Fox

Life of Sir Walter Scott – Lockhart

Writs of the Barony of Broughton

Scottish Record Office

Register of Sasines

"House of Commons 1754-90" – Sir Lewis Namier & John Brooke.

"North and South of Tweed" – Jean Lang

"Diary of John Campbell" (of the Royal Bank of Scotland)

Old and New Edinburgh – Grant

CHAPTER FIVE

CROSS KEYS HOTEL

"A charming scene of confusion; cooks, ladies' servants, waitresses all running against each other, being the time of Kelso Races. The company is composed of gentlemen of the Turf on both sides of the Tweed with families and friends and also members of the Caledonian Hunt. Foxhounds and harriers hunt alternately in the mornings. There is also a concert and races and next night the gentlemen of the Hunt give a handsome ball. After the ladies retired therefrom, the gentlemen formed a party to drink their healths and when I got up at 8 they were still drinking and meant to sit till hounds went out. This meeting, I heard, is most expensive of any. An English Steward was obliged to pay 10 guineas for his room, though only there 5 nights." So wrote Col. Thornton of Yorkshire after a visit to the Cross Keys Hotel in Kelso in 1786.

Kelso Races, on the flat, were recorded at Caverton Edge in 1735 and in 1751 the Caledonian Hunt gave a plate of 50 guineas as a prize. The course was over three miles of level ground, and the horses were generally stabled at Softlaw, about a mile away. The races quickly grew in popularity and by 1774 were described as a brilliant occasion, attracting members of the most noted families of the district including those of Buccleuch, Douglas, Ker, and Elliot. From the English side of the Border came the Delavals, Blakes and Northumberlands. In 1777, six years after Dickson's death, the Royal Caledonian Hunt was instituted and regularly made the Cross Keys Hotel their base for the occasion of Kelso Races. The gathering held various social events over two weeks, with a grand ball bringing the last day to a climax. As Col. Thornton indicates, some gentlemen celebrated throughout the night and climbed into the saddle for a day's hunting next morning! The Hunt consisted of 60 members, including 17 noblemen and 11 baronets, and their uniform was a scarlet frock-coat, green neck, plain silver buttons and a silver horn with a small gold fox on the left side. The horses had to be certified real hunters of the previous season, under the proprietors of the hounds with which they hunted. The entrance fee was 2 guineas, the winner to pay 1 guinea towards drums, colours and other expenses. Anybody wishing to erect a tent or hut on the grounds would be obliged to put 1/2 guinea towards the Plates; any disputes would be dealt with by the stewards. Races were always held in October, and in 1779 it was decided to have the first race at Kelso over 4 miles, the weight being 10 stone. Horses were entered at the Cross Keys.

In 1783 the stewards were Lord Elphinstone, Sir Francis Blake and Col. Wemyss and they may have been involved in the Hunt's invitation to Mr. Vincent Lunardi, the famous Italian balloonist who was secretary to the Neapolitan Ambassador in London, to come to Kelso in October 1785. As it took him three days to prepare for his "voyage" it is most likely that Lunardi stayed at the Cross Keys. He attended Kelso Races and watched as the Duke of Hamilton and Robert Baird rode their own horses and were obliged to race against each other a second time when the first ended in a draw (no photo-finishes then!) In the evening he was a guest at the dinner and ball which followed an exciting day. After his successful balloon flight to Doddington Moor and Baremoor, near Berwick, Lunardi returned to Kelso and the Cross Keys in triumph, bells ringing, drums beating and people cheering.

In 1818, the Duke of Roxburghe transferred the racecourse to Blakelaw, abandoning the grandstand and stabling which had been erected at Caverton Edge and planting the ground with trees. Bands of gipsies tended to make use of the disused grandstand for their midnight revelries, so it became known as "Baal's Altar", was regarded as an intolerable nuisance and pulled down by popular demand. The transfer to Blakelaw proved very unpopular. The races were finally moved to Kelso and the Duke erected a new racecourse and stand at Berrymoss, the foundation stone being laid on 12th July, 1822. The people of Kelso, recognising the value of the races as a financial asset to the town, contributed labour to convert waste ground into a reasonable surface for racing. By the 1860s, The Caledonian Hunt Race Meetings were being held in four different venues by turns: Kelso, Perth, Ayr and Edinburgh/Musselburgh; Stirling, Dumfries and Hamilton had been discontinued. In Kelso the racing stables were near the Square, adjacent to those of the Cross Keys Hotel, and the exercise yard for local horses was on the present site of the Tait Hall. The stables were tenanted until 1929 by Thomas Hardie and then by his right-hand man George Anderson, being known in recent memory as "Anderson's stables" and demolished in the 1980s.

The sign of the Cross Keys is ancient in origin, representing the arms of the Papal See and the emblem of St. Peter, tempting the speculation that this Inn existed from the time that the Abbey was occupied. In his "History of Roxburghshire", Jeffrey mentions a previous Cross Keys Inn

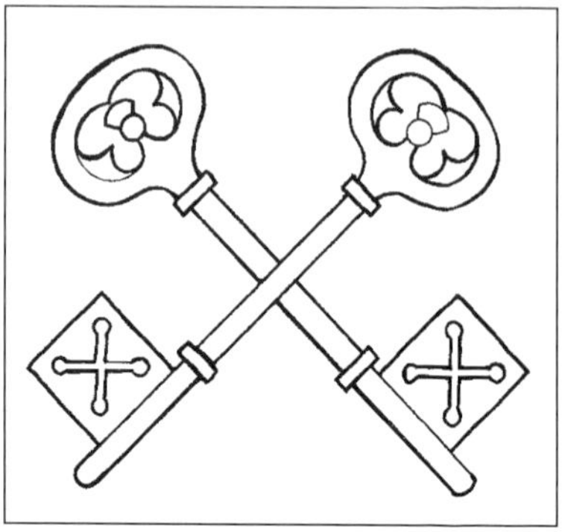

> *"on the site where Mr. Lindores lived, lately used as a post-office".*

Now this property was alongside, to the West of the present Cross Keys, and the proprietor was John Waldie, his wife Mary Clarke. He advertised in the Newcastle Journal in 1762 that he had procured four-wheeled post-chaises and assured his customers that the road between Newcastle and Edinburgh was now free of interruption because of the new bridge over the Tweed (finished in 1758). "Good chaises and careful drivers" could be hired at 9d per mile.

The map of fire-damaged properties, drawn up after the conflagration of 1684 in central Kelso, shows the area now covered by the Cross Keys as being owned by Nicol Park and Robert Ormiston, the latter a member of a well-to-do family. The Hearth Tax roll eleven years later gives the respective dues as one unit for Park and eight for Ormiston, indicating a large building. Dickson purchased these two tenements to the east of John Waldie's inn, each with "middingstead, back closs and pertinents", one of which had belonged to the heirs of Agnes Ormiston, widow of William, and the other to a later Robert Ormiston. To these he added a dwelling-house and shop and two back areas or yards with stables, barns and other buildings, which he bought from John Waldie of Hendersyde, and a small piece of ground which had belonged to Waldie the Innkeeper. (There were two John Waldies in Kelso at the same time, apparently cousins, which must have caused some confusion. John Waldie W.S. had married Jane Ormiston, who inherited Hendersyde). The minister of Morebattle, Andrew Chatto, had a preferable right to part of this property and he too sold to

James Dickson. The whole covered a fairly large area on the north side of Kelso's Market Square, in an excellent position for trade, and on this ground was erected the new Cross Keys Hotel with its extensive stabling. Like many other old properties around Kelso Square, the hotel has cellars which once travelled some distance underground, and a well, now filled in.

In 1766, Dickson was elected Royal Worshipful Master of Kelso's Masonic Lodge on St. Andrew's Day (November 30th) and retained this position until his death. The following year he offered the Masons a free meeting place in "a tenement he was then building", but it wasn't ready in time for the meeting on St. John the Baptist's Day in June 1769 and they met, at his request, in the Cross Keys Inn, which may still have existed next door. However, by November that same year they met in the Assembly Room as promised, indicating that the new Hotel was up and running. John Waldie apparently transferred as proprietor to the new Cross Keys, for in 1784 the "Kelso Chronicle" announced that George Horsington had taken over from John Waldie, but the latter had taken the Post Office with him from the hotel to his house at the foot of Oven Wynd. Horsington too was assuring the public of "neat post-chaises with able horses and careful drivers on the shortest notice". Robert Burns visited Kelso in May 1787 and dined with the Farmers Club and with Sir Alexander Don, whose brother-in-law was the Earl of Glencairn. The Earl was a member of the Caledonian Hunt and he persuaded them to subscribe en bloc to the second edition of the works of Robert Burns. A painting of the Square was done for Horsington in 1790, a time when most of the other properties around were rebuilt. This painting would have shown the old Town House, by then in a ruinous state, and possibly the pantwell which Dickson is supposed to have vandalised.

When George Horsington and his wife Betty Alexander left around 1796, Adam Main became landlord and "Mr. Main's ballroom" was used by Mr. G. Banks for dancing lessons; a grand ball for the scholars was followed by the Ladies and Gentlemen's ball, for which a band was engaged. Mr. Banks continued his dancing school for some years. Main was involved in the coaching business and in 1795 the ironically named "Kelso Fly", a slow, lumbering coach drawn by two horses, was leaving for Edinburgh twice weekly at 8 a.m. and arriving between 6 and 7 p.m., except in the winter, when the journey took 12 hours. A third horse was harnessed to expedite the journey, but it was still slow. By 1802, coaches left the Cross Keys for Edinburgh Canongate three times a week, departing at 7 a.m. and arriving at 4 p.m., the whole journey costing 13/-, or 4d per mile. The collapse of Kelso Bridge during a flood in 1797 must have been most inconvenient for coach journeys as the old ferry was brought back into operation across the Tweed and would have caused considerable delay. The replacement bridge, built by Rennie, was opened in April 1803 and acclaimed by the townsfolk – and no doubt by coach drivers! In May 1803, shortly before William Dickson died, Adam Main left the Cross Keys and sold off all the hotel furniture. He was still operating a 3-horse coach to Edinburgh, tickets from the Swan Inn, for 10/6 or 3d per mile, obviously desperate for trade.

Main was replaced at the Cross Keys Hotel by George Yule and his wife Mary. They had previously managed a Public House which also operated ferry-boats over the Tweed, but these became obsolete with the building of the new Kelso Bridge. The Yules had more recently opened a tavern called the "George Inn" at 5, Bridge Street, which was the former Ormiston mansion inherited by George Waldie of Hendersyde from his parents, John and Jane Waldie, and they hired out post-chaises with drivers. By this time, the ownership of the Cross Keys had passed to Sir Archibald Collingwood Dickson, son of Admiral William, who had inherited estate and property from his father, and the baronetcy from his uncle Archibald. Shortly after the Yules moved in, there was an unfortunate accident to a young man called Anderson, coachman to Mr. Rochester, one of the guests. The master's carriage was standing at the door of the hotel, when the horses took fright and bolted. Anderson clung on manfully and was dragged for 500 yards, but fell off and was trampled and run over, dying the next day. The horses had careered on for two miles before one of them fell. On a lighter note, the hotel's Assembly Room was the venue, in October 1803, for a concert patronised by the Earl of Dalhousie, of vocal and instrumental music on clarinet and violin, with Mr. and Mrs. Mahon performing.

There must have been considerable stir when the Volunteers, raised in 1794 against a possible invasion by Napoleon, were disbanded in the Square in May 1802 after an animated address from the commanding officer, Captain Davidson. Sergeant-Major Mabon was presented with a gold medal as a token of their appreciation. However, they were hastily re-formed at the end of

January, 1804, when one of the bonfires, set up to give warning of an invasion of the French, was accidentally lit and gave rise to the "False Alarm". The whole district was filled with volunteers marching to various rallying-points, including Kelso Square. Three companies of Kelso Volunteers, commanded by Sir George Douglas, "Captain" Waldie, the banker and "Captain" Robson lined up and cheered as their comrades arrived from the country.

George Yule was still landlord in 1807, when Sir Archibald Dickson was obliged to sell the hotel, for a price of £2,400, to cover debts affecting Ednam estate. The Town Council, or stentmasters, were complaining of being owed seven years' arrears of stent, or local rates, by the heirs of the late Admiral Dickson of Sydenham. They directed the Treasurer to

> *"transmit a statement of claim to the man of business of the Admiral's heirs* (George Jerdan)*, requiring immediate payment of the debt, or that an action will be raised against them for the purposes of liquidation".*

The purchasers of the Cross Keys were a consortium of four men: Thomas Nisbet of Mersington; John Murray of Uplaw; James Nisbet, tenant in Lambden; and Thomas Hood of Hardacres. A year later, George Yule borrowed £2,500 from David Fleming, smith and feuar in Kelso, and bought the hotel himself. He was described as a vintner, and his fellow-tenants were Charles Waldie, sadler and bailie, and John Rutherford, merchant. Witnesses to the transaction were John Waldie, Clerk in the Bank of Scotland, and William Dawson of Frogden, who was a famous agriculturist in his day. This was during the period when the succession to the Dukedom of Roxburghe, "heir of tailzie and lawful superior of the subjects", was under dispute and the estate was sequestrated until the 5th Duke inherited in 1812. The new Town House opposite the Cross Keys was erected soon after.

George Yule's sister-in-law, Anne Nicholson, who seems to have been residing with him, died in February 1811 and, perhaps realising that he himself did not have long to live, George drew up his will. He died on the 13th January, 1814, aged 52, leaving his widow Mary with a liferent in the hotel – as it turned out, only lasting four years. The Instrument of Seisen of 1816 was written by John Smith, writer and Baillie of Kelso, Charles Wilson, writer and his son Patrick, the apprentice. It was witnessed by Daniel McLeish, servant to George

Yule, and George Main, who was apprentice to William and John Smith, writers. William Smith had married Sarah Waldie and John was their eldest surviving son. John Smith had been Baillie during the confinement in Kelso of French prisoners from the Napoleonic wars (1810-1814) and was very popular amongst them because of his fair treatment. According to an observer, he was usually dressed in knee breeches and silk stockings. John lived in Abbey House, Bridge Street, later occupied by his brother, William, also a lawyer, who wrote articles for "Blackwood's Magazine".

Adam Yule, son of George and Mary, was 21 when he inherited the Cross Keys Hotel. Adam and a young woman known as Ann Hope had an illegitimate son, Thomas, in 1822 and it wasn't until 9 years later that Ann was restored to church priveleges and Thomas was baptised. In the meantime, Adam was married by Rev. Hunter of Oxnam to Elizabeth Elliot, whose family farmed at Hindhope, and they had two daughters – Mary, born in 1823 and Margaret, born in 1825.

Adam seems to have been an ambitious young man and he began to expand the hotel into adjoining premises. In 1822 he bought a new-built tenement called Tweed Lodge from John Gray, architect, of Harrietfield. This was located to the rear of the Cross Keys and behind the "King's Head Inn" in Roxburgh Street and consisted of a large public room or ballroom in the upper storey, a hayloft and schoolroom in the middle storey and 2 stables on the ground floor, with the midding-stead. According to a Kelsonian of the time, the ballroom was used as a banqueting-room and was adorned with landscapes by Mr. Hume, a local artist.

> *"These landscapes", in his opinion, "for breadth of design and delicacy of execution, for animation of fore-ground and softness that reposes in the distant perspective, have not been surpassed by any similar productions".*

John Gray retained the right to possess, either for his own use or for tenants, the northern stable on the ground floor for a period of 7 years. He also owned adjacent property fronting the Square, to the east of the Cross Keys, which at one time was run as an Inn by John Dodds. This he had purchased in 1814 from Thomas Dickson, son of Robert Dickson, wright, who had been the owner at the time when James Dickson made his purchase of tenements from the Ormistons, and raises the question as to whether there may have been a family connection.

John Wood's 1823 plan of Kelso shows that behind the buildings facing the Square (the name Market Place having been discontinued in 1797) there was a warren of lanes and closes intersecting a maze of randomly built dwellings. To the north of the Cross Keys lay an "interest and yard" belonging to John Crawford, merchant, which comprised a shop and dwelling-house. There was a lane (Jamieson's Entry, after a farm owned by John Jamieson, father of surgeon James Jamieson) running from the Cunzie Neuk, on Roxburgh Street, along behind the Cross Keys; a small passage between the Cross Keys and John Gray's tenement leading to the Square, and another from the start of Horsemarket through to the Back Way, later Bowmont Street. These lanes would only admit pedestrian traffic, so it was necessary for horse-drawn vehicles to pass right along Horsemarket before doubling back on Bowmont Street to arrive at "Mr. Hall's Meeting-House", where Trinity Church stands today. (Mr. Robert Hall was a Seceder and a famous preacher, who was succeeded by the equally well-known Rev. Henry Renton in 1831).

The Town Council of the day consisted of a Baron Bailie and seven stent-masters appointed by the Duke, with another seven representatives from the various Trades, and the Preses of the Merchant Company. The Bailie of Kelso in 1825 was Robert Bruce, writer; the Preses of the Town Council was Henry Swan; the Treasurer John Waldie. John Turner, slater, was deacon of the Hammermen and convener of the Incorporated Trades of Kelso. Other deacons included James Muir, Weavers; John Robertson, Skinners; John Scott, Shoemakers; Thomas Mitchell, Tailors; William Stuart, Fleshers. Alex. Blackie, sadler, was the Preses of the Merchant Company of Kelso. As these men all represented their trade, one must assume that the remaining members of the council were those appointed by the Duke, or, as he was a minor at that time, by his "tutors". These included William Clark, wright; John Gray, mason; Peter Ker, mason; Robert Williamson, druggist; William Elliot, architect; Andrew Lockie, nursery and seedsman; and Adam Yule himself. The stentmasters decided that it would be beneficial to form a road, 20' wide, giving vehicular passage from the Square through to the Meeting-House. Certain properties would have to be demolished and compensation paid, in addition to the cost of building, so a considerable sum was required to be raised by public subscription from the inhabitants of Kelso. (The number of stentmasters themselves involved in some way with the construction of this road gives rise to slight unease.) A special meeting was convened to arrange disposition of various properties, including one belonging to Adam Yule, and to agree on the closure of the passage alongside the Hotel, for which he was to receive compensation. His neighbour, John Gray, had died the year before, not long after the transfer of Tweed Lodge to Adam Yule, but Gray had left other properties which had been inherited by his son, the Rev. George Gray of Eckford. William Clark, joiner, John Gray and Peter Ker, masons, were to be responsible for forming the new road, and they purchased from George Gray prior to demolition. Property which Robert Bruce, the Bailie, had bought from George Sked, former baker, was included and he too was compensated with a payment of £245.3.2. A brick house formerly belonging to Peter Robertson was shut up as it was of no further use. The road formed at that time still exists, and is commonly called "the Dardanelles".

The "Superior of the subjects", Sir James Henry Robert Innes Ker, Bart. Earl and 6th Duke of Roxburghe, Marquis of Bowmont, Earl of Kelso, Viscount Broxmouth, Lord Ker of Cessford & Caverton, etc. was at this time only 9 years old, his father having died in July, 1823 at the age of 87. His affairs were being handled by his tutors, the Hon. Joshua Henry Mackenzie, senator of the College of Justice; John Fullerton Elphinstone, Esq., in the service of the East India Co.; Lt.-Col. William Keith Elphinstone; and Lt.-Col. James Drummond Buller Elphinstone. They appointed James Mackenzie, W.S. to handle the transactions with the stentmasters of Kelso.

It is to be hoped that the roadworks did not inconvenience the celebrations which took place in the Square on 12th August to mark the birthday of King George IV. A table "laid with wines" was set up in front of the Cross Keys and several prominent and respectable inhabitants were joined in drinking the king's health by members of the Bowmen of the Border. In the evening, a bonfire was lit in the Square, attracting youngsters who fired squibs. At intervals bells were rung, no doubt including the one in the dome of the new Town House. This bell was rung every week-day morning at 6 a.m. to call the inhabitants to work, and at 8 p.m. to retire. Although this must have been somewhat disturbing to the hotel guests, it may have been less so than the previous custom, when a piper and drummer paraded at 5 a.m. and 10 p.m!

The bond which had been agreed between George Yule and David Fleming was in 1828 transferred to their sons, Adam Yule and

Alexander Fleming who had followed his father's calling as a smith. It would appear that Adam Yule had never actually paid John Gray for the tenement known as "Tweed Lodge", for in 1829 he borrowed money to pay for it from Miss Gershoma Hannah Wallace, younger daughter of the Rev. Gavin Wallace of Nenthorn. Yule's solicitor, Patrick Wilson, wrote to John Smith, W.S., acting for Rev. George Gray:

> *"In consideration of your having delivered up to me the disposition by the Rev. George Gray, minister of Maybole, to Adam Yule, vintner, of that large tenement at the back of the Cross Keys, I oblige myself to pay into your cash account with the Bank of Scotland this day the sum of £420, being the price of the said large tenement, with £22.0.8, being one year eighteen days' interest due on the said principal sum".*

Seven years passed and still Adam Yule had not complied with his obligations. In 1836, he acknowledged the loan and agreed to insure the tenement for not less than £450 at the Sun Fire, or some other respectable insurance office. Miss Wallace had married her father's successor, Rev. Gifford, in 1832, and perhaps her husband insisted that Adam should repay the money. In December 1836, the messenger-at-arms, Andrew Drysdale,

> *"passed to the Market Cross of Edinburgh and, after crying three several oyesses, open proclamation and publicly reading the written letters of horning and the said execution in His Majesty's name and authority lawfully denounced him (Adam Yule) H.M.'s rebel and put him to the horn by three several blasts".*

This did produce a result, in that Adam Yule paid £50 on account and a further £25 in 1842.

The Cross Keys, from the time it was built, was at the centre of Kelso's life as a town and its importance grew as time went on. People frequently referred to it when giving directions – "Mrs. Stuart's in the Horsemarket, only 6 doors from the Cross Keys"; "George Humble, cabinetmakers, moved to Brisbane Place, near the Cross Keys". The passing coaches had increased in number, with daily services to Edinburgh and London and to local towns as required. Fares on Post coaches from Kelso to London were £4.10.0 inside and £2.7.0 outside; from Kelso to Newcastle cost £1.0.0 inside and 12/- outside. The Tweed and Clydesdale Union coach to Glasgow cost £1.4.0 inside and 16/- outside. For those who could afford the extra, a seat inside was infinitely preferable, particularly in winter, when some passengers had to be helped down, frozen into immobility. What a welcome sight the Cross Keys must have been on those occasions! Friday was market-day in Kelso, and on that day there might be over 6,000 people milling around Kelso Square, buying produce such as bread, butter, cheese, vegetables, fruit, poultry and fish from the various stall-holders. The arcades under the Town House were used for this purpose, but the rest of the week they were merely collecting areas for refuse and a source of complaint. On Fridays, five coaches left the Cross Keys at the same time, adding to the bustle and general excitement of the hectic day; it must have taken considerable skill and care to negotiate a team of four horses safely through the crowds. Friday was also Hiring Day and in Kelso these occured on the first Friday in March for hinds, and the first Fridays of May and November for young men and women. The Horse Fair was held on the second Friday in March and the Wool Fair on the second Friday of July. The Cross Keys Assembly Room was in constant use for a variety of purposes, including sales of household furniture for those moving house on Hiring Days.

The bond for £2,500 which Alexander Fleming held from Adam Yule was sold on in 1841 to three men – George Watt, John Robertson and Thomas Wood. George Watt was a merchant, well-known in Kelso; John Robertson was a perfumer; Thomas Wood a millwright. In January, 1849, George Watt died and the other two decided to pass the bond to John Romanes of Lauder, the transfer being corroborated by Adam Yule. John Robertson was so blind and frail by this time that he was unable to sign; Thomas Wood departed for Manchester shortly afterwards.

The railway came to Kelso in 1850 and this entirely changed the transport system of the country. Coaches became almost redundant overnight, but Adam Yule began to operate a horse-bus to take people to Kelso Station, which was temporarily situated at Wallace Nick, on the road to Jedburgh, before moving to its final site in Maxwellheugh. A party of the "Free Gardener's Society" of Edinburgh took a rail trip to Kelso at this time and made their way from Wallace Nick to the Cross Keys, where they "partook of a hearty breakfast".

Another person hiring the Assembly Rooms, in November 1851, was Mrs. Leighton from London, who gave a lecture on "the advantages of Bloomerism". Mrs. Leighton dressed in the Bloomer style, which was felt to be superior to the current mode of female dress. She wore a green silk dress, the skirts of which reached a little below the knee, the upper part reaching the throat, with wide trousers drawn together at the ankle. Over this she wore a close jacket of dark crimson velvet, trimmed with black lace fringe, and on her head a broad-brimmed hat with feather. In this attire she lectured to a small audience on female costume through the ages, and the evils of tight-lacing. Alas for Mrs. Leighton, she was ahead of her time and wrote, in an article to an American journal, that had she foreseen the notoriety and ridicule which she had incurred, she would never have commenced the movement.

After the new road, now known as "the Dardanelles", was finished in 1828, Adam Yule bought a piece of ground from Clark, Gray and Ker, the constructors. Twelve years later, he sold it, with a stable, to John Dagg, residing at Kielder Castle, Northumberland, Thomas Elliot, tenant in Hindhope, a relation of his wife, and James Elliot, tenant in Molehaugh *(sic)*. For some reason, there was an agreement that it should be resold to Adam Yule for £80, and this was done in 1853. John Dagg was now living at Knoppings-holme, Northumberland, and his servant, Andrew Charlton, was among the witnesses to the sale.

The next year Adam Yule died, aged 57, insolvent. Because of this, a petition against Elizabeth, his widow, and his daughters was presented to the Sheriff of Roxburghshire at the instance of several writers and trades-men in Kelso. By this time, Adam's daughters had both been married: Margaret to Thomas Penny, farmer at Bartlehill, and Mary to James Darling Wilson, writer, son of Patrick Wilson. The Wilsons had resided at Sydenham before going to live in Garryduffe, near Ardfinnan, Co. Tipperary. The Sheriff was asked to authorise a proper person to take an inventory, sell perishable effects and let the Hotel. Robert Curry, of the Swan Inn, was appointed Trustee with the consent of Adam Nichol, merchant, Alexander Elliot publisher of the Kelso Mail, and Thomas Kennedy, coach-builder.

In the meantime, life at the hotel had its ups and downs. The Bowmont House Seminary, a School for Girls run by Miss Paterson, held a very successful exhibition of work in the Tweed Lodge room. And a Hungarian band under M. Kalozdy, accompanied by Madame

Bellosio and Miss J.Z. Mein, gave a concert. There was near-disaster when fire broke out because a candle was placed too near bed-hangings and they, the bed-clothes and the bedstead were all badly burned. Luckily, the hotel staff managed to extinguish the flames before the fire spread, but not before several inhabitants turned out in answer to an alarm raised by "tuck of drum". During September 1854, at the height of the turmoil caused by public outrage about the continuing unjust toll on Kelso Bridge, 200 special constables were sworn in. They were formed into divisions in the Cross Keys Assembly Rooms to be addressed by the Duke of Buccleuch.

In April 1855, Robert Curry exposed the hotel for sale by public "roup", or auction, during the running of a half-hour sand-glass, with George Main acting as judge. The upset price for the 17-bedroom hotel, two shops, dwelling-houses, stabling for 50 horses, and Tweed Lodge was £4,400, but there were no offers. The following month it was again put up for sale, at a reduced price of £3,550, but without success. Meantime the tenants were allowed to stay on. These included Robert Forsythe, the head waiter, a native of Coldstream, whose wife Jane was barmaid at the hotel and Robert Rathie, who operated a stabling and coach-hire business. A range of stables with garden or yard, east of Bowmont Street, were put to roup and purchased for £370 by Patrick Wilson on behalf of John Bulman, joiner. Eventually, in December that year, the hotel was purchased by Robert Romanes on behalf of John Romanes of Lauder, who already held a bond on the property. Tweed Lodge was bought by William Robson, W.S. on behalf of Mrs. Gifford, to whom the Yules still owed money.

The new manager of the Cross Keys was George Oliver, who transferred from the Spread Eagle Hotel in Jedburgh, which was the regular venue for meetings of the famous Jedforest Club. George was accompanied by his wife Euphemia and son George, who later ran the hotel himself. Robert Forsythe remained with them as head waiter until the next change of management. Once again, a branch of the Post Office was incorporated into the hotel.

In 1859, John Romanes drew up a will, with disposition in favour of his wife, Isabella Mason. The trustees were: Robert Mason of Herriotshall; James Curle, writer in Melrose; George Henderson of Huntlywood; Thomas Henderson in Boon (who went to farm in Shidlaw, Northumberland); Thomas Simson of Blainslie and Rev. Charles Simson, who later went to Van Diemen's Land.

Postcard of Cross Keys Hotel, 1904

James Keddie became landlord of the Cross Keys in 1867 and obviously upset quite a few local people by his actions, for he prevented access to adjacent properties from the east side, which had been available from time immemorial. The Red Lion Inn was situated behind the hotel and its landlord, Alexander Buddo of St. Andrews, was prevented from using the stable which he rented from Mrs. Gifford. Peter Croall and Sons, coach-builders, were also tenants whose ingress was obstructed and Mrs. Gifford suffered loss of income as a result. By 1870, Mrs. Gifford had had enough and took an action against James Keddie. The Sheriff ordered him to allow access, to pay compensation of £10 and expenses. The Census record for 1871 shows that James Keddie was born in Crailing in 1816, while his wife, Caroline, had come from Surrey. Their daughter Sarah, 16, had been born in Dumfriesshire, while their twelve-year-old son James was born in Brechin. David, the eldest son, was not included in the Kelso Census and perhaps had already moved to Edinburgh, where he was married in 1878.

Two years later, Mrs. Gifford, now a widow, moved to Dalgan Park, Co. Mayo and gifted Tweed Lodge to her daughter Anne. James Keddie bought the building from Anne in 1876 and the following year bought the Cross Keys itself from the heirs of Mr. Romanes. He proceeded to make alterations to the French style of double roof to accommodate a promenade and added an Italianate facade. Because the Kelso Races were no longer the grand occasions of previous times, the Assembly Rooms were converted to increase bedroom accommodation.

Visitors to the hotel were never short of entertainment, for the Square was in constant and varied use. In March, 1889, they would have been confronted, on leaving the front entrance, by the faces of "Brutus" the lion and "Princess" the lioness peering through the bars of their cages, for Bostock and Wombwell's Menagerie was in town. Since 1850, when it was just Wombwell's, the menagerie had afforded people the opportunity to view a large collection of wild animals, whose presence was heralded by a brass band to draw the crowds. Queen Victoria's birthday was celebrated in May 1889 with the usual bonfire occupying the space in front of the hotel, the heat on some occasions being intense enough to crack the window-panes. That year, however, the heavy rain literally put a damper on things; the fireworks display was abandoned and the fire was left to burn away unattended as the revellers retreated to the warmth of home.

James Keddie died in 1889, leaving the Cross Keys property to his three children. David Keddie now lived at "Froylehurst", the Friars, Jedburgh, where he operated the Friars Burn Brewery. Sarah Keddie had become Mrs. John Watts and lived in London, while James Thomas Keddie remained in Kelso and bought his sister's share in the hotel. He was proprietor when Beatrix Potter stayed at The Cross Keys with her family in August, 1894 and recorded in her journal that it was "large and dingy". When James T. Keddie died in May 1917, the children of his brother David inherited, their father having died in 1900. James' nephew, James David, had emigrated to Canada and joined the 48th Canadian Highlanders at the outbreak of the first World War, being wounded at Ypres in 1915. Initially taken to the military hospital at Boulogne, he was transferred to the Royal Hospital at Huddersfield and had his right foot amputated due to injury by an explosive bullet. The delay he experienced in getting an artificial foot was raised in parliament by Sir John Jardine, M.P. for Roxburghshire. James was anxious to be fitted with a prosthesis to enable him to visit his mother in Jedburgh, before returning to Canada. His sister, Edith, was married to a pencil-case manufacturer in Birmingham and neither of them was interested in retaining ownership of an hotel in Kelso. Their aunt Sarah Watts repurchased the Cross Keys and it was she who entered into an agreement to lease the stables to William Service, postmaster, of Simon Square. Mrs. Watts sold the Cross Keys in 1922 and it had a chequered career until it was most recently purchased, in 1975, by Mr. Kenneth Ballantyne.

At the time of writing, the Hotel is managed by Mr. & Mrs. Marcello and Susan Beccatelli and continues to be a natural focus for incoming visitors as well as Kelso's community, more than two hundred years after James Dickson bought the "tenements and midding-stead".

CHAPTER FIVE - SOURCES

"The Border Tour" by "a Tourist" (John Mason)

"Kelso Races" – J. Fairfax-Blakeborough

"History of Kelso", 1825 – Haig

Annals of a Border Club – Tancred

Kelso Stent Masters' Records

Kelso Mail – 1802 and various

Kelso Chronicle, 1783 and others

"To move with the Times" – Anne Gordon

Register of Sasines

Census Records

Lunardi Aerial Voyages in Scotland

CHAPTER SIX

EDNAM

The parish of Ednam, lying just over two miles north-east of Kelso, takes its name from the small river, the Eden, which flows through the attractive village of Ednam a short distance before it joins the river Tweed. From Kelso the road approaches Ednam across a neat stone bridge, with the old mill buildings over to the left, the crow-stepped gables of Eden House in the foreground, and a blacksmith's smiddy to the right. Turn left over the bridge and the road to the

Ednam Cottages, 1948

church and its walled kirkyard lies between two rows of neat cottages set behind gardens filled with flowers. These are the brick cottages with slate or pantiled roofs built by James Dickson, very much in the same style as those of Broughton, and as little changed in two hundred years.

Ednam's known history began in the days of King Edgar, second son of King Malcolm and his Queen, Margaret, when a Barony was created in the gift of the king. At the beginning of the twelfth century, Edgar gifted Ednam to his Norse friend and vassal, Thor Longus, who founded a church there in honour of St. Cuthbert. At that time, and for centuries after, the land around Ednam was peat bog and wilderness, but Thor attempted to improve it by endowing the church with a plough. Succeeding kings granted lands in Ednam to the monks of Coldingham and Kelso, and the right to use the mill at Ednam if their own should not be in working order. In 1314, the year of Bannockburn, the lands at Ednam were forfeited to the crown, and Robert Bruce settled them on his daughter, Marjorie. She married Walter Fitz-Alan, Lord High Steward of Scotland, and they founded the Stewart dynasty, their son becoming King Robert II. In 1374, Robert sent ambassadors, including Sir John de Edmonstone, knight, to Charles V of France, to solicit his intercession with the Pope. John Edmonstone was a descendant of Edmond, a Saxon follower of Queen Margaret said to be a younger son of Count Egmont of Flanders, who gave his name to Edmonstone, a mile south of Niddrie, where Edmonstone House was built.

Robert III gave Ednam to his sister Isabel, Countess Douglas, widowed when Earl Douglas was killed at the battle of Otterburn, on the occasion of her marriage in 1392 to Sir John Edmonstoune. The Edmonstounes were lairds of Ednam for many generations, and built a castle, a tower and a double vaulted steeple which were "cast down" by Lord Dacre on his invasion in 1523. However, the tower and steeple were mentioned in title deeds of 1787, so must have continued to exist in part until that date. The Edmonstoune mansion house was later converted into a thrashing mill, standing on the farm of Ednam West Mains. Besides the Barony of Ednam, the Edmonstounes owned the ancient Hospital, which is commemorated in the Spittal field opposite Kelso race-course, and the lands of Bernington, Barlies and Berryloch lying between Ednam and Kelso. They also had the farms of Kaimflat, Newtonlees, Harpertoun, Highridgehall and Edenmouth, formerly called Earnslaw, where there were fishings and a ferryboat. These farms were sold to the neighbouring landowner, Sir Alexander Don of Newton Don, whose daughter, Isabel, married Andrew Edmonstoune. By the middle of the 17th century, the family was running into financial difficulties and various individuals held mortgages which brought them an annual rent from Ednam estate.

The minister at Ednam in 1692 was Rev. Thomas Thomson, son of a gardener to the Edmonstounes, and one of his kirk elders was John Cooke who married Jean Duncan of Smailholm in January, 1693.

The following year a son, James, was born to John and Jean and he eventually moved to Ayton and thence to Martin Cleveland where his son, also James, was born in 1728. The younger James Cook joined the navy and found fame as a navigator and explorer. In 1769, Captain Charles Douglas (p. 30) had been ordered to observe the transit of Venus from the North Cape of Lapland; Captain Cook was ordered to observe the same planet from the Pacific. Venus was due to transit the Sun – an event which would not occur for another 100 years. Astronomers hoped that by observing this transit from various points of the world, they would obtain an accurate measurement of the distance between the earth and the sun. Cook travelled extensively in the Antipodes until 1779, when he was murdered in Hawaii.

Rev. Thomas Thomson married Beatrix Trotter of Fogo and in 1700, just before they moved to Southdean, their son James was born at Ednam manse. He achieved fame as a poet, writing the well-known "Seasons" while acting as tutor to the family of Lord Binning in Hertfordshire. In London he attracted the notice of the Prince of Wales, who made a handsome settlement on him. In August, 1748, Thomson became overheated on a walk from London to Hammersmith, then chilled while sailing in a boat to Kew, dying shortly after. At the instigation of the Earl of Buchan, a monument in the shape of an obelisk was erected on Ednam Hill to his memory in 1820 by the "Ednam Club", and still stands today. The right-of-way leading to it became known as the "Tirlies", after the large turnstiles which took the place of gates or stiles across the path, between the fields.

James Edmonstoune, grandson of Andrew and Isabel, became the seventeenth laird of Ednam in 1760 and he sold what remained of the estate, removing to Corehouse near Lanark. The Register of Sasines records that in March 1765, James Edmonstoune of Ednam, Esquire, heir to Andrew, his brother german, (who had predeceased his father) sold "the mains of Ednam, 7 mark lands called the West end, parts of the Barony lying south of Eden, 15 single lands of the East end of the town of Ednam, and Ednam East Mains, then known as Cliftonhill, 2 cornmills, lands and mansion" to James Dickson of Broughton. Dickson also bought the bonds which were held on the estate by Sir Alexander Don, Sir James Nasmyth of Posso, M.P. for Peebles-shire, his brothers Robert and John Nasmyth, and Kenneth McKenzie, Lord Fortrose. From now on, he would be known as James Dickson of Ednam.

Ednam, 1886

In addition, between Ednam and Kelso, he acquired common ground known as Lillie Loch; fields in Bernington from John Lillie, feuar in Kelso, and 11 acres from John's son William. Several well-known families including the Chattos, Ormistons and Waldies owned land in Bernington, which seems to have been quite an extensive area. By this time, John Waldie W.S. was laird of Hayhope, Berryhill and Bernington and, like several others of the Waldie family, he married an Ormiston. Charles Ormiston, Quaker, owner of a mansion in Bridge Street adjacent to Ednam House, was a merchant who traded with Holland and at times acted as a money-lender. He died during the fateful year of 1684 and his son, also Charles, added to his wealth in 1699 by purchasing the estate at Spittal through his solicitor, Charles Waldie. In 1715 the Ormistons bought the estate at Hendersyde from the Edmonstones, but even in 1745 when the Highland Army came foraging there was still a wide area of bog-land on which very poorly nourished livestock scraped an existence. Gradually the land was drained and improved and a fine house built, containing a library which was later put at the disposal of the young Sir Walter Scott. John Waldie and Dr. William Ormiston of Hendersyde also sold part of their lands in Bernington to James Dickson. William Ormiston's sister Jane married John Waldie the laird in 1749. As a Quaker marrying outwith the faith, she was obliged to write a letter which was read out at the Kelso Meeting House, acknowledging that her marriage was contrary to the rules of the Society. When Dr. Ormiston died in 1771, his sister Jane fell heir to the estate and she and John became known as the Waldies of Hendersyde.

There had also been frequent inter-marriages between members of the Ormiston and Chatto families over the years. Andrew Chatto, minister at Morebattle, was the son of Thomas Chatto of Mainhouse and he inherited several properties in Kelso as well as parcels of land including part of Bernington which he too sold to Dickson. At Eden Water, Dickson purchased from Robert Happer, baxter, 5 acres and grass ground and from Thomas Fraser, merchant, 7 riggs of outfield, all on lands known as Gowdsknow (or Gowksknow). James Dickson formed part of this land into one farm and built a farmhouse, naming the whole Sydenham. His other land purchases were sporadic but legion and extended from Ednam right into Kelso.

A linen industry flourished in the Borders in the 18th century and had been carried on at Ednam, originally by Dutch weavers who wove fine cloth, but later using Irish methods. Scottish linen was exported to the colonies, particularly to America and the West Indies, for clothing slaves. Samuel and Peter Robertson were sons of Quaker Samuel Robertson who, like his father Thomas, was a gardener at Bridgend (later Springwood) in Kelso. They were involved in the linen industry in Kelso and in 1740 Peter, then aged 21, was sent to Glasgow for instruction. There was a bleach-field near Broomlands in Kelso in the area now occupied by Inchmyre, and also at Ednam, where one of the fields was known as "Wash-house field". Every piece of linen which was offered for sale was inspected and stamped, both to establish the length of cloth and to protect the buyer. The linen woven at Ednam was stamped with the thistle in Kelso. It is possible that James Dickson promoted business opportunities for the local industry in his trade with the West Indies.

Another of the Robertson family, David, had a brewing business in Kelso probably at a site identified in a later deed as being in Mill Wynd and described as "a large dwelling-house, brewery, cellars, stables and other buildings", bounded by Kiln Wynd. David Robertson also had a son called Samuel and James Dickson is supposed to have offered them the opportunity to move their business to Ednam and so reduce the tax bill imposed by the stentmasters.

Eden House and Ednam Brewery

The machinery of Ednam brewery was driven by a head of water from the mill cauld, which spanned the Eden a little way above Ednam Bridge. Initially, the Robertsons lived in a cottage now known as Ednam West Mains farmhouse until the Brewery House, now named Eden House, was built beside the bridge and occupied by Samuel and his wife Margaret, sister of John Robertson who later lived at Ednam House in Kelso. Samuel accompanied Robert Burns to Dunbar in 1787 – Burns refers to him in his diary as "Mr. Robinson". A remarkable tree, a wych-elm, grew in the garden of the Brewery, recorded in 1859 as measuring 23' in circumference, 60' high and with branches spreading for a distance of 23 yards! The Robertsons were very successful in their brewing business and exported ale and porter in large quantities, much of it to England. There seems to have been a certain amount of home consumption too, for the Census of 1841 mentions three alehouses in Ednam – mostly patronised by Kelsonians!

In the year 1764, just as James Dickson was negotiating the purchase of Ednam, the minister, the Rev. Thomas Pollock, died. Mr. Pollock had come from Paisley in 1722, presented to the church at Ednam by the King, but resented by the local lairds and heritors. Patronage was generally resented at this time, and Mr. Pollock was involved in a well-documented incident in Morebattle in 1725 when the Duke of Roxburghe imposed his choice of minister on the people, who showed their disapproval in no uncertain terms; a riot ensued at the attempted induction and Mr. Pollock fared rather badly. There were many Seceders in Ednam and they were obliged to register births in the parish register held by the Established minister, but they considered the tax on baptism a "profanation" and often didn't bother complying. The kirk and manse at Ednam were needing to be replaced, and in October 1755 a committee was appointed to view the proposed building site. Mr. Andrew Potts attended, representing the Heritors whose responsibility it was to provide funds for the fabric of church and manse. They included Sir Alexander Don, James Edmonstoune, John Waldie and Charles Ormiston who, according to Rev. George Ridpath of Stichill,

"were very little disposed to do anything obliging to Mr. Pollock".

This latter observation seems to have been a shrewd one, for two years later nothing had been done and the kirk had been lying in ruins for almost 3 years. Workmen gave estimates on oath that about £147 was needed for the work. Three more years later, the situation had become grave and a charge of horning was to be executed against the Ednam heritors for repairs to the manse which had been too long delayed. In 1759, The Presbytery ordered that a new kirk should be built and a new site was agreed on by the Court of Session, although all the dimensions were smaller than they should have been for the size of the congregation. Again the materials were the subject of disagreement – Don and Ormiston thought that the old materials should be used, while Edmonstoune went further and declared that **any** would do. Action was at last spurred and the work commenced in 1761, although a large part of the materials were of low standard and the total cost when work finally went ahead was £163. The church so cheaply built for Mr. Pollock's congregation lasted less than 50 years and in 1802 it was replaced by the present one, well-constructed by a Kelso joiner called Robertson.

Thomas Pollock had many vexations to contend with. He had the right to graze a horse and it was transferred daily to each of 5 farms belonging to Sir Alexander Don, in rotation. One of his cows grazed on Ednam pasture and the other on Hendersyde. However Ormiston of Hendersyde, who was after all a Quaker, decided that he would cease the practice and instead the minister would be given £20 Scots, (£1.16.8 sterling) in lieu. This bargain, poor as it was, was never fulfilled and a dispute ensued, during which the minister went unpaid. Not unnaturally, Mr. Pollock complained to the

Presbytery, rather rashly declaring that the whole parish was kirk land! At the end of 8 months the decision was given – return to alternate grazing.

In November and December 1764, the vacancy in Ednam Kirk pulpit still unfilled, the Rev. Robert Hogg of Roxburgh and Rev. Andrew Chatto of Morebattle, Moderator, preached to the congregation. In the same month, March 1765, that James Dickson completed the purchase of Ednam estate, the Rev. David Dickson was appointed by the crown. Although he bore the surname of the proprietor, the two don't seem to have been related. David Dickson was born in 1720 to George Dickson and Catherine Hamilton at Whitehill, Earlston; he died unmarried in 1795. He was remarkable for the amazingly ornate capital letters with which he began the minutes of the Presbytery, to which he was secretary, as Mr. Pollock had been before him. The Presbytery seemed willing to take up Rev. Dickson's case regarding the grazing of his animals and found that his glebe was the minimum required and that he received far too little for his animals' grazing. Although they were prepared to tackle this problem on his behalf, he requested a delay and the matter was never settled. The Kirk Session minutes give an interesting inventory of utensils held by Ednam Kirk in 1782: *3 mortcloths – 1 little, 1 very old, 1 tolerable; 1 long table-cloth in very bad order; 1 small tablecloth – tolerable; 4 cups, 5 flagons, 3 plates; Bason for Baptisms; Bag of Tokens; 1 old chest in bad order, wanting a lock – new one to be ordered.* The locks and snecks were mended by Edward Fairbairn, the blacksmith. Rev. Dickson wrote the first Statistical Account of the parish in 1793 and he reported that the population of Ednam at that time numbered six hundred, having grown from the 387 recorded in Dr. Webster's census of 1755. He described the roads as very bad, repaired by Statute labour, and with tollbars established by Act of Parliament.

The schoolmaster was also new to his post. John Weir married Jannet Huet in Ednam in 1764 and they had a family of 12 children. According to Burleigh, writing in "Ednam and its Indwellers", John Weir (he calls him James) was a poor schoolmaster who "frequented taverns and ale-houses".

James Dickson's dream was to connect Kelso and Ednam to the seaport of Berwick via a canal. He began by building a mill at the upper end of the village, fitted with machinery of "the approved type" and manned by workmen from Yorkshire (the county where his brother Archibald lived). Once this was operational, he sought financial investment in his canal and called a meeting of local magnates, but had to abandon the project due to lack of enthusiasm. The mill became well-known for the production of English blankets and woollen cloth.

At the end of 1770, James Dickson sold part of Ednam estate known as "the Lobby" on the west side of the house which had been built on the foundation of Ednam House barn, with adjacent stables, byres and houses; together with enclosures called Clover Park and Midpark, formerly possessed by George Brewes; Graymansfield on the north side of the new main road; and Broompark possessed by John Gray with houses and yards. The purchaser was Sir John Paterson, Baronet of Eccles, son-in-law of the Earl of Marchmont, a gambling man universally disliked. This transaction was witnessed in London by James Dickson's nephew, Lt. Archibald Dickson, and his friend Albert Innes of Crutched Friars. In some unexplained way, this same property was disponed by Walter Scott W.S. to James Dickson in June 1771 and "seised" by William Dickson in 1787.

Captain William Dickson inherited the remainder of the estate at Ednam when his uncle died in 1771, settling at Sydenham with his wife Jane after the house at Broughton was gutted by fire, and several of their younger children were born there. Having sold Broughton, he applied to the Court and obtained the authority of an Act of Parliament. This was entitled "An act for empowering the judges of the Court of Session in Scotland to sell such part or parts of the Estate of Ednam in the County of Roxburghshire, formerly belonging to James Dickson and now to Captain William Dickson as shall be sufficient for payment of debts affecting the same as the said decreet of sale and lands and others therein". William proceeded to sell in 1787, at the time of his second marriage, when he appears to have been settling a great many of his affairs. The new owner of Ednam estate was Mr. Arthur Cuthbert of Madras, East Indies and later of Woodcotpark in Surrey, who was succeeded by his son, James Ramsay Cuthbert in 1792. Cuthbert bought Ednam House itself from "Captain William Dickson, R.N., late of Ednam, now of Sydenham".

[An intriguing entry in the Ednam Kirk accounts of 1790 records that alms were given to 7 sailors in distress; 7d in April and 6d in September. Were these sailors connected to Admiral William Dickson, and if not what were they doing in Ednam?]

Walter Scott, W.S. survived his client James Dickson and in 1776 he purchased about 3 acres of park and enclosure near the Tweed from John Waldie of Hendersyde, trustee for Thomas Thomson, merchant in Newcastle. Then, in 1779, he further purchased property in that part of Ednam which still belonged to Mrs. Jean Waldie. This was known as Newstead, and consisted of "houses together with $^1/_2$ teinds, parsonage and vicarage".

At Ednam West Mains, in 1793, there resided an army officer, latterly a lieutenant in the Roxburgh Cavalry Fencibles under Sir John Scott of Ancrum, called Thomas Lyte. Thomas and his wife, Anna Maria, had a son in June that year, christened Henry Francis, and another, George John, in March 1795. The Lytes are recorded as attending St. Andrew's Chapel in Kelso until 1798. Henry Francis Lyte became a clergyman and famous as writer of the popular hymn "Abide with Me".

Meanwhile, Samuel Robertson continued to brew beer until his early death in 1807, when his body was conveyed to Kelso for burial in the ground belonging to the Society of Friends in the Knowes (he was later re-interred in Ednam kirkyard). His son Peter, only 21 when his father died, left the Quaker faith and was baptised into the Kirk at Ednam. He carried on the brewing business and a year later had to contend with a fire in the brewery which was brought under control by the villagers, who rallied round and formed a chain to pass buckets of water. Peter Robertson was the eldest of nine children, the next three brothers all dying at an early age; Peter was eight years older than his brother Samuel and eleven years older than Alexander and therefore had to act as a substitute father. Alexander attended Jedburgh Grammar School under the tuition of Mr. William Lorrain, whose reputation seems to have been greater than that of the Kelso headmaster, George Gillies. In 1814 Peter wrote to Mr. Lorrain expressing pleasure at the latter's report of Alexander's good behaviour but lamenting his bad scrawl! Peter Robertson moved to Harpertoun as a farmer in 1818, then to Newtonlees, with his wife Agnes Nisbet. His uncle John Robertson, brother of his mother, married late in life and bought Ednam House in Kelso in 1818. John Robertson took a keen interest in the welfare of his nephews and nieces and mentioned them in his will. Peter's brothers David, Alexander, and Samuel all died abroad, the latter in 1838. His youngest brother, Archibald Shaw Robertson, went to

Capetown for some years and there his daughters were born, but he returned to finish his days living in Duncan House, Kelso. By that time Peter Robertson had also moved into Kelso, buying "Newarth" from Dr. Charles Wilson when the latter moved to Edinburgh in 1853. His wife, Agnes Nisbet, died eight years later and his son Peter inherited Newarth on his death in 1871.

Ednam Brewery remained deserted until its next tenant, Peter Nichol of Kelso took over in 1833. Following Nichol there was a succession of operators until John and William, sons of John Murray and Margaret Galbraith, took over in 1877. John Murray junior had been trained in the science of brewing, but he died within a year of practising his art, at the tender age of 29. His father died two years later and William Murray was left to carry on alone until 1885, when the Brewery again took fire, but this time the villagers laboured in vain to save it and the business was abandoned. William went to a Brewery at Craigmillar in Edinburgh and prospered, a "Wee Murray" becoming a favourite drink.

One of the Ednam stories to be handed down describes how a bucket of ale was fetched from the brewery every day to be hung in the blacksmith's workshop. Men who were waiting for their horses to be shod could pay 1d for a mug of ale and help themselves from the bucket. The smiddy was occupied by Fairbairns for generations until the last Edward Fairbairn died in 1916. They were followed by Bob McCraw; he handed over to the Rennies and Arthur Rennie, now retired, still lives with his wife in Ednam Cottage.

In 1827, Ednam estate was bought by Viscount Dudley and Ward, Foreign Secretary in the Government, who became Earl Dudley and Viscount Ednam. On his death 6 years later, his cousin, Rev. William Humble, inherited and was known as Baron Ward. His son, William, regained the titles of Earl and Viscount on his succession in 1836 and made one visit to his estate at Ednam. None was made by his son who became Viceroy of Ireland and, having no interest in his Scottish inheritance, sold it in 1904 to a descendant of John Waldie and Jane Ormiston of Hendersyde. Their son George had a daughter, Maria Jane, who married Sir Richard Griffith, Bart. In time Maria and Richard had a son, George, who inherited Hendersyde and became Sir George Waldie-Griffith; his son Sir Richard John Waldie Griffith was born in 1850 and followed a military career, retiring shortly after his marriage.

Although Admiral William Dickson sold the Ednam estate in 1787, he did retain for himself the property at Sydenham and to it he took his new bride Betty Charters to live with the five children from his first marriage. William and Betty proceeded to have six children of their own, James being the eldest, born in 1788 and Louisa the youngest in 1796. By now, William was an Admiral of the Blue, he was 66 years old, and spending a good deal of time at sea. His eldest son, William, had married his cousin Elizabeth, daughter of Sir Archibald, had joined the army and had died in active service in 1795. Archibald Collingwood Dickson had followed his father into the navy and received his first Naval Commission in 1791 as Lieutenant on the flagship of Sir Alexander Hood, enjoying rapid promotion and making Captain by 1799. He inherited the baronetcy from his uncle and the property at Sydenham after William died in 1804, but seems to have spent little time there. However, he enlarged the bounds of Sydenham by purchasing the adjoining farm of Kaimknowe, also known as Pylestead. When Sir Archibald Collingwood Dickson 2nd Baronet, rear admiral of the red died in June 1827 he was succeeded by his eldest son, William, who was born in 1798. William also went to sea and became a Rear-Admiral reserved, retiring from the navy in 1825. His main residence was at Hardingham in Norfolk, inherited from his father and his great-uncle Archibald, but he was a magistrate for Roxburghshire. In 1832 he sold Kaimflat to Robert Thomson of Lauder, a draper in the Lawnmarket in Edinburgh and in 1868 the farm was absorbed into Stichill estate when it was purchased by George Baird.

Sir William Dickson, 3rd Baronet, married late in life to Miss Northey of Pembrokeshire and they had no family. In 1864, by arrangement with his brothers, who were to be his heirs, Sydenham was disentailed to get rid of the clause about the designation "Dickson of Ednam" and then re-entailed on the same heirs. When William died in January, 1868 his brother Colpoys, Col. in the Hon. East India Company's service, succeeded to the Baronetcy and to Sydenham on the death of William in January 1868. Five months later he too died, in Folkestone, and the property passed to their younger brother, Alexander Collingwood Thomas Dickson, 5th Baronet, who survived until 1884. His nephew, John Poynder Dickson Poynder, inherited Sydenham but was a military man and M.P. for N. W. Wiltshire, having little contact with his Roxburghshire seat.

In 1904, Sir Richard Waldie Griffith added Sydenham to Hendersyde and became laird of Ednam. He improved the row of cottages in Ednam built by James Dickson, adding the storm windows with Gothic pinnacles and making the interiors more comfortable. He also built the delightful school which is still in use today, contributing much of the cost from his own pocket. In September, 1948, Ednam Estate was sold in lots in the Cross Keys Hotel in Kelso on behalf of members of the Bedington family. On the morning of the sale, individual tenants were given the opportunity to purchase the property they occupied, and many did so. The two rows of cottages, however, found no immediate buyers and were offered for sale at £100 each! Post-war villagers were unable to take advantage of a bargain.

The little road between these cottages leads to the entrance to Ednam churchyard. Just inside, on the right, stands the memorial to James Dickson, "late merchant in London and representative in Parliament for the district of Peebles", the stone sadly flaking into obliteration. How little it tells us of a remarkable man, whose talents and enterprise are still benefiting the population of his native district.

James Dickson's Tombstone at Ednam Church

CHAPTER SIX – SOURCES

Ednam and Its Indwellers – Burleigh

Diary of George Ridpath

Register of Sasines

Old Parish Records

Old and New Edinburgh – James Grant

Rutherfurd's Southern Counties Directory

Scots Magazine

History of Roxburghshire – Jeffrey

One of Zion's Gates – Donald Gaddes

Ledger of Ednam House Trust

INDEX

Family Trees:

ACKNOWLEDGEMENTS

During the preparation of this book I have had generous help, some of it considerable, from various individuals. I would like to convey my heart-felt thanks to them all and hope the following list omits none:

Mr. Ian Abernethy, Heiton, Kelso

Mr. Kenneth Ballantyne, Cross Keys, Kelso

Mr. & Mrs. Marcello Beccatelli, Cross Keys, Kelso

Mr. & Mrs. Alastair Brooks, Ednam House Hotel

Miss Roz Brown, Archives, Selkirk

Sir Ilay Campbell, Bart., Crarae

Miss Helen Darling, Archives, Selkirk

Rev. David Edwardson, St. Andrew's Church, Kelso

Mr. Andrew Elliott, Broughton Place

Mrs. Elspeth Ewan, Yetholm

Mr. Hector Innes, Kelso

Dr. Michael Robson, Isle of Lewis

Mr. Andrew Fox, Broughton

Mr. & Mrs. David Lyell, late of Ednam

Mr. & Mrs. Arthur Rennie, Ednam

Mrs. Jane Robson, late of Yetholm

Mrs. Anne Scott, Walton Hall, Kelso

Mr. James Stenhouse, Kelso

Mr. James Stewart, Kelso

Mr. Denis Sweenie, Ednam

Members of Staff at Taits, Solicitors

Mrs. Sandra White, Kelso